Gifts from God are daily earned.

Given equally to all mankind.

Gratitude embedded in all received.

Granted to you for good deeds returned from being kind.

Addictions A to Z:

Alphabet Soup Bowl

Poems by
"Tiger" Lydi Pallarés

Edited by
Karen and Dennis O'Donovan

Library of Congress Cataloguing-in-Publication Data

ISBN 978-0-9967750-0-7

Editors: Karen and Dennis O'Donovan
Publisher: Teach Me Tech LLC
Cover Design & Typesetting: Dennis O'Donovan
Manufacturing: Lulu Publishing

Cover - Star Field image courtesy of spacetelescope.org.
Back Cover - Photo courtesy of Carol Pattison.

Acknowledgements

First I want to thank my parents, Mathias Frederick Charles Burggraf and Helen Elenor Burggraf for endowing me with their genetic codes – including my dyslexic traits – that granted me unique and uninhibited perspectives on using words. This gift also taught me the courage and tenacity to tread into the unknown.

To my brothers Robert George Burggraf and Edward Mathias Burggraf, for respecting me being there for them as their guiding elder sister.

To my daughter Lolin, who loved me and encouraged me to rise above and survive chaos and blockades. I forever will remember her kindhearted spirit and radiant smile.

To Laura, my daughter, who remains unpretentious and nonverbal in her inventions and ideas until she has successfully proven them. She is creative, and most loving and kind.

To my grandsons: Bobby, who just graduated in 2015 with honors from Vanderbilt; and Gianni, who is in his third year at Johns Hopkins and is on the Dean's List for two years straight.

To my youngest, Vince, who showed me what courage really is; and to his dear wife Linda and to my newborn granddaughter Lee.

Thanks to Boston's famous Coach Bill Squires, a former All-American runner and former Olympic running coach. Bill and I share weekly phone calls, discussing my book projects and his upcoming biography. His jokes and stories keep me laughing and smiling. Bill called me "Tiger" when he coached me as an ultramarathon runner. I lived up to that name when I ran 105-plus miles in a 24-hour race in Rhode Island. I won that race and broke U.S. and world records.

My thanks to Carol Pattinson, for the flattering photo of me on the back cover.

Thanks to Ginny, my A.A. sponsor of 31 years, who kept believing in me and kept me sober through many heartbreaks and crises.

Kudos to my editors, typists, publishers and friends Dennis and Karen O'Donovan. Poor Karen had to decipher my all-capital, badly typed and mostly misspelled words, turning a manuscript full of errors into properly typed poems. It must have been like translating a foreign language for her and Dennis. My book was formatted by Dennis who had to learn how my dyslexic mind works, with all the offbeat formatting and creative spellings I envisioned. I owe them thanks from the whole of my heart. This book was made possible by their guidance and never-ending hard work...and their belief in me. They brought out my Sagittarian "flaming fire" and ignited it for the world to read.

- "Tiger" Lydi Pallarés

This book is dedicated to
Lolin Lee Elena Pallarés
8/19/70 - 3/30/07

Gravesites in South Miami, FL and Brickenridge, CO
Lolin's star coordinates:
Ursa Minor Ra 16th 52m 408 D88'14'

From Liz to Lolin, My Best Friend
2007

A special day for all of us 37 years ago

when our friend Lolin was born in the city of Chicago.

She had a smile on her face and mischief in her eyes;

the fact [she] came from Lydi was really no surprise.

Two years later Laura would arrive as cute as she could be,

quite possibly the reason Lolin didn't carry a dolly.

The family moved down to Virginia by 1970.

Before Lolin turned four, little Vincent joined the family.

Six more years would pass before we would get to meet.

I knew almost immediately this girl was really neat!

Our neighborhood was great – kids were everywhere –

but once I met Lolin, we became a pair.

When Lolin began to blossom she was certainly a ten,

but her smile's what we loved to see over and over again.

High school was a challenge;

lots of laughs and lots of tears.

Before long I got married to a guy named David G.

It was Lolin who brought us together when we were just 13.

While I had the boys and worried about raising a family,

Lolin went to college to earn herself a degree.

The list she had of boyfriends could go on and on.

Not that much later Ricky came along.

"Let's move to Colorado"- together they would dream;

little did she know what that dream would mean.

The impact of the West was made upon her tender heart.

She fell in love with the mountains from the very start.

X

When the couple parted ways, Lolin had a special friend

even though it took some time for their hearts to mend.

The friends Lolin made in Colorado became oh so dear.

When she came back to Florida it was hard to not have them near.

The ocean called her back to us much to our delight,

but we knew in her heart it was a bit of a fight.

Marriage found her in Florida; it can be quite the fashion,

but saving all those animals was really her true passion.

She worked so hard to save each and every soul,

finding them a loving home was her ultimate goal.

Alas, soon divorce took its toll.

Lolin was brave and strong for those who couldn't do.

It's no doubt she was a Leo, a leader through and through.

Going through this lifetime making her own path,

never stopping to worry about taking someone's wrath.

She had always been my angel looking out for me.

She saved my ass many times when I was up a tree.

I love her like a sister — everything I'd share.

To have a friend like her is really kinda rare.

I'll sum things up by saying how fortunate we've been

to have Lolin spend time with us, to have her call us friend.

LIVE - LOVE - LAUGH - DREAM - BELIEVE

Liz Ginsberg

Table of Contents

Chapter 1

Alcohol And Drugs

Addiction of Alcohol and Drugs

Awaiting you is your alluring addiction

Always been waiting for you to try

Anxious to get you high.

Aiming for someone new,

perhaps you...

adolescent,

teen,

adult,

senior.

Alphabetically from *a thru z,*

alpha begins,

zero ends.

Part One - Babies

Alas, addiction can be passed to a babe in mother's womb.

Abdomen cradling the embryo swimming,

twirling,

whirling,

swirling in genetic fluid.

Alternation or damage likely by addictive abuse

Awash with what mother has digested

Also by ingestion from drug and alcohol use

Addiction may take its destructive tow

Arriving alive by birth upon this planet earth.

Afterbirth expelled and umbilical cut and tied first.

Awesome newborn ...yet time will tell

if the precious dear is well.

Foretold,

Forewarned,

Foredoomed?

Aware of facts that drugs and alcohol spell hell!!!

Part Two - Pre-Adolescents

Any one of any age may become addicted

Any time, anywhere alcohol or drugs exist

At home, at the playground, a child can be set adrift

Accepting a freebie gift:

> if only to sniff
>
> if only to taste
>
> if only to try
>
> if only then to die.

Awesome aftereffects created desire for more

Ambushed one more child to the *"new candy store"*

After a free sample, craved it and now dearly paid

Allowance saved to pay the drug dealer.

Asking price was too high.

Answer was to steal,

> swipe,
>
> burglarize,
>
> snoop and loot,
>
> deal and wheel.

Antidote needed for one so little.

Afraid you're an addict, kiddo!!!

Part Three - Teens

Alphabet for teenagers

   formulated with every letter,

   some worse, some better.

   Oh, so many pages!

All the A's to Z's are seriously mixed up

   in a jumbled time!

All you can imagine and more in this time line!!!

Add your own words and experiences as they change all the time!

Part Four - Adults

Affected by alcohol is affirmative

Awesome how in drunken denial they live.

Autobiography based on omissions

Abstinence not their life's missions

Abuse was their choice of positions

Adding chemical addictions

Absorbed in lies of fiction

Apologies in diabolic disguise

Aspirations were left far behind.

Aspirins or blackouts are warning signs,

Along with bloodshot eyes.

After a bender, can't walk the line.

Afterward an arrest is made.

Adult behavior needs psychiatric aid.

Analysis, an alternative for every liar.

Alas, aging doesn't make one wiser.

Part Five - Seniors

Amateur drinkers decades ago

After all we were younger then....so

Angelic,

        optimistic,

        dramatic,

And definitely an addict.

Amigos at the bar drinking,

        no rational thinking,

        so stinking.

All of us on social security or a pension.

Although, it's barely too little to mention.

Address is here, with many a beer

        and no tension.

Agenda is against an assisted living cage.

Absent from a dementia stage,

        just overlook my age.

Adios to Addiction

A dios to alcohol and drug addiction!!!
Alphabetical versed from a to z to capture

each in a chapter.

Raison d'être only.

No bogus bologna.

No friction fiction.

No magic potions used,

nor doctor or nurse.

Totally unrehearsed to attack your drug curse

of use and abuse,

before you dangerously get worse.

Alcoholics Anonymous is a proven source;
Assistance by others to aid and support you to quit.
Advice is only for assisting you, of course,

to abort your deadly habit.

or "have it your way!"

All alone or with the help of those in A.A.
Alternate programs and rehabs also exist
Any which way, but aspire to sobriety each day.
Annihilating all your past rhinoshit!
Ambitious achievement will test your wit.
Aim is to see a complete recovery.
Assuredly you'll then lose the past pain

And gain...a new world of self-discovery.
Abstinence is your gift earned by being sane!
Awarded for your life anew!
Add sobriety to your bucket list.
Abolished is rhinoshit you won't miss.
A kiss to Avatar of todays so new.
Adios! Adieu! Arrivederci! Auf Wiedersehen!
Addiction is through!
Alas, be aware--it will always be awaiting,

    baiting

        enticing,

           tempting,

             lurking,

                sneering,

                  snickering,

                    stalking,

till..................

                    stalemating.

till.............................

                      successful.

    Until you're spinelessly seduced

        or goosed.

ABC

Adios Alternatives

A la carte

Self-service

Alternatives available are:

arrested	- **a**. arraignment
ambulance	- **b**. body bag
asylum	- **c**. crazy
addiction	- **d**. death

Battle with the Bottle

Battle with the bottle again?

Broken promises of quitting never end,

Again, you're on a bend.

Boozing,

Babbling,

Bitching,

Begrudging,

Slurring,

Staggering,

Scandalizing,

Scoffing,

Suffering,

Spinning,

Sputtering.

Bona fide drunk is the message you send.

Bartender is your best friend,

Servicing…

Supplying…

Pouring you more and more, with no end.

Pleasing you as much as he can.

Plying you with alcohol's poison nonstop.

Perhaps to get safely home is the best opt.

But, nope, on a bender once again.

Blame the booze, it's always the same!

Bottoms up, gulp it down, getting drunk is the aim.

Bury all your woes, goblins and griefs

Bar room brawl lurking, awaiting

Booze aiding and waiting

Blackout banishes a blitz

Bedlam denied, for tonight

Bash time is gone, so is sanity and wit.

Bummer, you shouted...no brawl,

Between heaving and weaving,

Barely able to crawl.

Burst your bubble, buddy... can you think?

But truth is you're sick and stink!

Brewery breath smells foul...wow!

Best to sleep it off!

Bottom line, too much booze!

Brutal cough too...as you snooze.

Bucket beside your bed...

Enough said!

Busting your gut with regurgitating all night.

Barfing after dawn's bright light.

Blackouts are a prime interval in your life time.

Prognosis postulated:

Physiologically unstable!

Plastered patient,

Puking blood,

Pacemaker stopped,

Paddles prolonged,

Physician proclaims patient passed.

Body pronounced brain dead- -- - - - - - - - - -

Postmortem,

Pallbearers,

Mourners.

Bereavement ...bemusement...

AHA...Beneficiaries!

Birth

We all begin dying within seconds of birth.

Unknown is our time frame here.

Placed in mother's care

Maternal love is there.

First we learn to crawl

        and then walk on planet earth.

You are embraced in her arms

           and closely held,

       sheltered from worldly harms.

Newborn tears wiped from chubby cheeks.

Your hunger satisfied by mother's breasts.

Once home, all becomes a series of new tests.

Learning to crawl and showing off your best.

Dear mother rarely could rest.

Before long you learned to smile.

Pampered you were with no denial....

Journey is always a lifelong trial.

Later you started to walk and talk... and talked...

When displeased ...you bailed and balked

       not knowing of life's fears and tears;

       life's real tears follow in years.

Mother's lessons were put to tests.

Advice from her was wise!

Based on truth, not on lies,

　　　　　nor on fairy tales in disguise.

Teenager, but still growing more wise,

Mom's facts stayed the same.

Drinking, smoking, drugs: just say a flat out no!!!

　　　　　best not placed in my **alphabet soup bowl!**

Life is not a game!

　　　　　Wise wisdom was her goal.

Addiction always awaiting...

　　　　　baiting its abusive toll,

　　　　　to capture you causing endless woe!

Ascribing to mothers warning words

Angels and I shout no.....no.....no way!!!

　　　　　Go away!!!

Mother taught me well of words to say

From her past yesterdays to today.

Truly spoken, mother's mistakes she did tell

Wrong footsteps once led her to a living hell.

My alphabet soup bowl was magic since my birth

Warning me, beware, on this planet earth.

Only heed words of true worth

Awareness of those deeds will keep me well!!

Placed true words into my bowl

Containing my heart and soul.

Those can't cast an evil spell!

Bottles Galore

Bottles galore of swigging beer or liquor,

Back to back nonstop.

Both resulting in a bibulous stupor,

    ending in a super-duper hangover.

Bender was a beast,

Blame it on *Bacchus,* your benefactor.

Barfing night and day, it did not cease.

Besotted boozer!

Behind blood-shot eyes,

Bottles galore of swigging beer or liquor,

    You broke the boundaries again.

Beyond into bankruptcy of your heart and soul,

Beware, you're really a loser!

Before, you promised it would end.

Bragging, boasting you'll ban the booze.

Bandwagon begins, but always you lose.

Blackout lingers around the bend.

Believe in yourself and restore your health,

Break the bottle to stop your *rhinoshit!*

Be brave... be bold...just do it!

Benefits will follow a billion fold, so told.

Become a sober bedrock for inspiration.

Blessed with a source of admiration

Bizarre behavior before; now a blank page.

      Sobriety sets you free to script a better life.

Before you... is yourself anew!

Better and better as you age.

Bondage to ways before was of old.

Behind you was the pathetic you.

Before you is your life, brand new.

Carnival Time

Carnival time is party time.

Casual substance abuse in use.

Carousel ride begins,

      who knows when it ends?

Crackerjack act you lack.

Craving drugs back to back!

Caboosing around the bends,

Chugalugging alcohol down.

Crack too is around,

Celebrations abound.

Children say —not cool!

      look like a fool.

Compulsion of using and boozing,

      riding a merry-go-round.

Courtship is of drug using.

Certainly abusing isn't amusing!

Curving,

      up and down

        round and round

          swerving nearer to the ground:

    swallowing,

      slurring,

mumbling,

tripping,

falling,

tumbling,

cursing.

Choices were unsound.

Comatose in the carousel

Cycle of puking!

Critique is, you're not well,

looking like hell!

Circling around and around,

up high then down,

down,

down,

down

Crashing!

Crashed on your ass!

all has come to the past.

Curiously asking, at last,

Choose one as your last task:

cremation or crypt?

Cordial courtesy for those who wept.

Cut the Crap

Cut the crap!!!

        fess up and take the rap!

Confirm the admission of your addiction!

        self-abusive of your prescription.

Confront the real fact.

Cut out the noncommittal act.

Continued to cheat by using cocaine.

Clandestine behavior, clever and sly...

causing family shame and pain

        lie, lying, liar...

        'til you die!

        how insane!

        only you're to blame!

Coincidentally: coke, crystal, crack, cocktails, cognac

        all are the same.

        all clinically attack.

Continual consumption will end life's game.

Confessed that your addiction is true.

Choosing drugs you constantly pursue.

Checking out whatever is new

        indulging in every other.

Cunningly too,

                    your drug use you cover.

Cyberspace is your central core.

Caused by your chemical addiction.

Cannabis smoked more and more.

Clinically classified and certified

                    as a user and boozer.

Circumstances created collisions with companions.

Complacency led to job insecurity or worse.

Cursed when fired due to your alcoholic thirst!

Confirmed as a conniving loser.

Conscientious objector in your boozing war

Consequently, no one can help you anymore.

Caduceus climaxed in an overdosed cadaver.

Crib to cremation...

Cold destination is your end of creation.

Denial of Addiction

Denial of your addictive using or drinking

                always your repeated motto.

Dreadful stinking thinking!

Declaring you only have a wee bit of "it."

Damnable *rhinoshit!*

Drank straight out of the bottle

                        left it empty as it could be.

Drugged, drunk, or doped is just the same.

                  You do it every day,

                     always your own way!

                          you have a lying dishonest aim;

                              never do you admit any shame.

Damnation! Rhinoshit!

Definitely I will not remain in your game!

Dawn to dusk, it's always the same:

                you sneak and seek someone to blame.

                it's so insane!

Darling, your excuses are so very lame.

Deliberately, deceitfully, you use others.

Deception is your middle name.

Dilemma is: I'm overwhelmed and smothered!

Drafted my views and list of why I'm so pissed.

Drastic is your addiction, so, please, read my list.

Download it to your heart and mind.

Dearest, I love you, but divorce papers I will sign!

Dilemma is no longer debatable, I find.

Detailed list is as follows:

detached

deviant

depressed

defensive

difficult

disagreeable

decadent

declining

downhill

disconnected

disengaged

dispassionate

disorientated

drinking...

drunk...

drugged...

or soon dead?

detox needed!!!

Driving Drunk

Drinks...

Drunk...

driving!

Dead drunk...

D-e-a-d!

Drugs Trials
and Horrific Errors

Tell me I can try it just this one time

     Only once, that's all!

Just want to know what it's like

     to feel the sublime...

A high... like a climb up tall mountain peaks

     to the top of the world.

A high... like I've never known before

     to soar thru the clouds like a kite

     to feel peace within my right for one night.

          Yes, my child, I will be your best friend.

          I will give you the experience of a lifetime.

          You will remember it without an end.

          Try your choice this time.

          Come with me, join the crowd.

          Your friends have tried many.

          Now it's your turn, you're allowed.

          First timers get to pick any.

          I'll become your best friend

          to the very end.

          I'll guide you through the trials.

          I'll show you the greatest love of all.

I'll be watching all your smiles.

Your problems will be vanished.

All worries will disappear.

All are banished.

Try it, just try it once.

I'll be right here...near.

Your free choice:

> swallow it,
>
> smoke it,
>
> snort it,
>
> shoot it up,
>
> inject it.

It's your private choice.

Listen to my voice!

First drug is free.

It's on me, you see.

No strings attached.

There's no catch to buy.

Pick out the one you want to try.

Go ahead, then take another one.

You are akin to me, as my son.

Can't decide?

Should I be your guide?

Try this one first, then the others

Just like your friends and fellow brothers.

That's the way to go, my child.

Liked it, didn't you?

You say you want more?

It's your choice.

I'll always be here offering more anytime.

But--this time, it will cost you plenty!

Give me your money and your life.

Give me every waking moment of it.

You belong to me now!!!

There is no escape!!!

"I am drugs" and I own you forever

from dawn into the dark abyss of night.

Your thoughts will dwell on me,

Even when out of sight.

Forsake your parents and every friend.

You belong to me now without end.

Forget those you loved before.

You now love me more.

Vanished are your future plans and dreams.

I captivated you and won the addiction war!

Can't escape me with all your horrific screams.

You are mine, for my name is *"drugs."*

I am your worst nightmare come true.

At all hours you will crave.

'til you will collapse into your grave.

You will long for our moments together.

Do recall, you allowed me to lead you here

to the fairyland of addictions.

My child, you're here to stay.

No escape...no way.

You're imprisoned in powder, weed, or liquid.

Just by trying only that one time,

only once it took.

Thereafter you became hooked.

I waited patiently for your decline,

after the first time...

you soared sky high and wild.

You destroyed not only your life, my child,

but those who loved you were left behind.

Banished all to sniff the trail of your white line.

In the passage of time, you'll remember your vow.

"Just wanted to try drugs only once!"

*Y*es, just one time...

it took to cross the line!

Drunk Driver

Drunk as a skunk!

        punk.

             gentleman.

                   teenager.

                        lady or man.

Don't you understand?

Drunk driver leaving the bar

        driving a car.

Decreased abilities, deficient facilities.

Dedicated driver not behind the wheel.

Dangerous road ahead!

Deprecation of reflexes...

        A—Auto askew...annihilation

        B—Braked, but blitzed by booze

        C—Crisscrossed cross walk...crashed

        D—Demolished! Deadly destination

Devastation by one drunk driver.

Dozen died, save one survivor.

Drastic disaster, disembodied or disabled.

Dipsomaniac addict was among the dead.

        E—Enough said!

Easy Escape

Easy way to escape from living life,

        just choose an addiction.

Evaporating your problems with drugs or alcohol.

Escaping from the facts of life with booze;

Exempting you from the truth.

Every day a new excuse to use, to abuse.

Elaborate excuses given are just another extravaganza.

Elixir you envisioned is just a prediction,

        but only is pure fiction.

Examine your martini glass,

Empty to the last drop.

Endeavor not have one after the other, does not last.

Each glass refilled then emptied again, for you can't stop.

Eliminated your problems and demons through your addiction?

Experiment of using was a failure,

        a falsehood

        a foist

        a fantasy

        a fiasco

Egocentric behavior exposed.

Everyone knows for it shows.

Embedded enmeshed in your mind.

Ejection of your super ego; jettison this time.

Evinced evidence to walk a straight line.

Emerging effort for sobriety begins a new life.

       Beginning,

           entering,

               entertaining,

                    embarking,

                        embracing,

                             enriching,

                        empowering

                  enhancing,

              enlightening,

                    enrapturing.

Emotions stabilized... no longer in turmoil.

Expurgated from addiction's grasp.

Extensive sober extraordinary experience is a life's task.

Excrement of the past has been cast.

Eruption from your abscessed ass.

Exorcised it indelicately at long last.

Exemplifying to stay clean is my high priority!

Evacuated all *rhinoshit* to join an ethereal society.

Father

Standing alone in this world I can't deny.

Father left me without saying goodbye.

Before then he deserted everyone

Using drugs and booze he chose, ignoring me.

He lived his life as a user and boozer.

Left life as a loser.

Longing to hear his voice again

                    drunk or sober

Yearning for his embrace

                    even though he died in disgrace.

I prayed he would quit!

I pleaded to him to cut out that rhinoshit!

                    sometimes he did for a bit.

I begged him time after time.

                    did he ever hear me?

                    did he see me sobbing?

                    did he even care?

Drugs or alcohol were always there

                    everywhere

                    in his hands

                    cans by his side

                    here and there

I tried so hard to get him clean and sober.

That task never came to pass,

                  never would last.

What more could I do?

With him vomiting bending over

Why did he not try to help himself?

When downhill went his health over years,

Alcohol and drugs were only what he wanted.

Knew I was invisible to him and felt haunted.

Felt unwanted and alone through my tears,

I thought how much went unshared.

Had he ever cared?

Drunk from morn or noon,

Passed out in the dark of night.

Awoke to drink more to dawn's first light.

Recovery he never even tried.

Begged him that I would be at his side.

Yet death claimed him too soon,

Leaving my heart with an unhealed wound.

Sobbing under a blackened moon of gloom.

First Love's Power

First love...

        'til forever.

First sip...

        for forevermore.

I hug you close to me...

        never will I let you go.

I embrace you tight and tighter...

        always together until I die.

First drink became my greatest love.

I adore and love you, not knowing why.

Never will I leave you,

Just us two, below and above.

No one else may enter.

No others may come between us,

        my dearest love.

No other love fulfills my being.

You are my life's center:

        no other

            nor sister

            nor brother

            nor mother

            nor child

            nor spouse

nor friend

father, daughter, or son

I depend on you for each breath I take.

I will not forsake you even at the end...

Yet, I wonder, do you love me for my sake?

Why do you laugh,

then turn your back?

Desolated then...

left alone... forgotten... how I ache!

My life you did take between my sips.

When liquor first moistened my lips,

You kept me begging on my knees,

Drunk and torn apart... you did tease.

You wrench my heart and soul,

from head to toe.

I beseech you...let me go!

Alas, I know I can't live without you.

Seduced me with your magical power.

You surround me with drugs

That I taste and not to waste.

Addiction owns me every day and hour.

36

Footsteps of Genetics - The Journey

Mom and Dad and your Grands

gave you their DNA gifts.
Your inheritance of life on planet earth
Formed from your very birth...

earthling genes,

not alterable,

yet...outcome's changeable.

ancestral footprints leading your way...

each and every day,

adding your own markers

with each step.

Baseline genes are encoded:

eyes brown as mother earth...

or of blue water...

son or daughter.

Walking in their path

which you at first followed

in a winding,

spiraling pace.

Father led the way yesterday.
But no longer will today.

37

Footsteps of drunkenness,

staggering,

downward falling,

passing out,

blacking out.

Sons or daughters born from mother's womb,

mom now guides you from each morn

to the setting sun.

Years went by.

You grew.

Then you knew

To look up at the sky

Where tears are falling down.

Misled steps, now you know why

one does cry.

hear the weeping sounds!

Father's life style is of alcoholic denial.

Genes already in place, from day of birth.

Born of mother earth.

Dad I must ask,

Is my passage in life shadowed,

and my sunshine stolen,

by your addictive habits?

Good Intentions

Each day give to someone a smile

By giving someone a ray of your sunshine.

Just by being simply kind

It will brighten their day.

you'll be enlightened along the way.

Living in sobriety will escalate when you share;

when to others you show you care.

If you're thankful to be "dry" inside you,

when outside be it sunshine or stormy rain.

A day sober or clean is a day of rainbows;

sharing, caring will take away pain.

Sunlight shall penetrate your every pore

deep into your heart's core.

Clouds of gloom or remorse dissipate when sober.

Darkness is no longer surrounding you.

Gifts to others make you feel new.

Clear head and heart

Now that's being smart!

Hangovers

Happy Hour tonight.

Heavy duty using and drinking;

Hesitated to drive...just too tight.

Hungry thirst for the toxic liquor.

Hallucinated 'til dawn's light.

Huge headache and got sicker

Hated to face the morn.

Hung over, puking, stinking

Hippopotamus shit pile taste

High-fived me in my face.

Hightailing it home at last

Her highness will be full of sass,

Homicidal and waiting to kick my ass.

　　　　Hah...you're home at last!

　　　　Here you're drunk again!

　　　　Hear me! When will it end?

　　　　Hobbling and wobbling,

　　　　　　staggering.

　　　　Harebrained husband tell me when!

　　　　Hardly able to walk or talk.

　　　　Heaving in the commode

40

from mouth to ass.

Hedonism and your foul breath and gas.

Having one drink after another.

Hands still grasping a liquor glass.

Hypnotized by drugs and booze.

Hooked! You drink and use.

Habit you have is.... Addiction.

No, rhinoshit!!!

Honestly, can you quit?

Hundreds of times you swore you stopped!

Historically, you drank and used 'til you dropped.

Heaving in the morn still.

Health going downhill.

Hate to tell you but you look ill.

Heart attack may be lurking.

Hysterical, yet still smirking.

Havoc you cause me, I swear.

Have to suggest you need medical care.

Halfway house, hospital or a rehab!

Howsoever--just get well or go to hell!

Here's my ultimatum deal:

Hear me, don't come home 'til you heal!!!

Hangovers are gone

Hyped up on drugs too long.

Heaving up, all are to be left behind.

Heed what I say and walk the line.

Helplessly still drunk today?

      then head for the highway!

Hate to say

      Divorce suits me fine!

Heartbroken but sick and tired of your hell.

Harsh measures I demand:

Hereafter I prefer being alone

      on my own.

Hunch...you'll soon ask for a loan.

Horse feathers! I won't even toss you a bone!

Honky-tonk bar brim filled with liquor.

Hocked all you had for a drunken weekend?

Henceforth: **Mr. Ex** "The loser boozer"

      get lost!!!

Hear me clearly, now I'm my own boss!!!

Huh! Isn't that the grand "kicker"?

Hate you and your damn liquor!

Helter-Skelter

Have been there;

  Done that before.

Hooked on drugs and more.

Had fallen into my abyss.

Hitting a low bottom...sinking

  By using,

  By abusing.

However, hindsight challenged me to make a list

  Changing me to care,

  And becoming aware ...

Horrific distress and heartbreak, to others

  I had caused,

  By my habit of using.

  By my habitual abusing.

Hangovers swirling into maelstroms from boozing.

Handicapped medically, no longer amusing.

Halfway house now, seems appealing.

Hallucinations are haunting.

Harmony in life needs a safe harbor.

Hades luring me, if I don't quit.

Helter-skelter am I!

Help is what I seek, I don't want to die!

done with my rhinoshit!!!

I will not lie.

nor ask why.

rehab needed, I won't deny!

Interplanetary

Internationally incalculable people are alcoholics.

getting high for kicks

Interplanetary beings probably do not do, too.

Intelligent humans of this blue planet earth do.

Interstellar beings likely to have strong convictions.

In absentia from their home; yet without addictions.

Impulsive mankind offenses against each other,

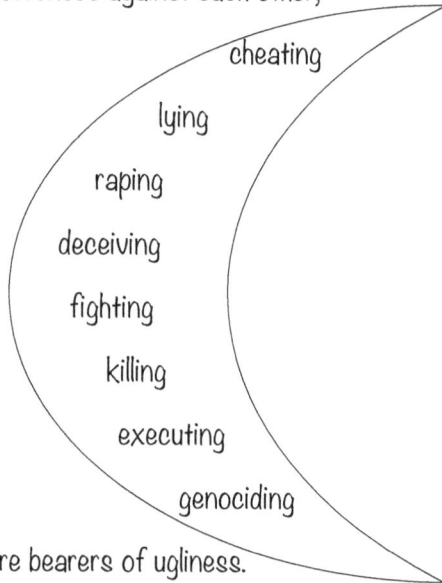

cheating

lying

raping

deceiving

fighting

killing

executing

genociding

Inhuman acts we are bearers of ugliness.

Impeccability is not within us.

Imperfections are we get drunk and cuss.

Improbable that aliens could ever be like us...

Juveniles on the Loose

Juveniles on the loose...

        sipping potent juice.

Junior's slurring his words after its use...

        youth on the loose!

Joyriding in Dad's car.

Jagging a drinking spree

        snagged his key.

Just driving nearby, not too far

        we'll be back in a jiff!

        if...

        all goes well...

Joints we'll light up to share.

Jam-packed car; opened the windows for air.

        we're almost there.

Jaunt for more beer and liquor to buy.

Just to get high as a kite in the sky.

        if...

        all goes well...

Jived and bribed the jerk inside.

        job done...liquor sold.

...all went well!

Jitterbugged out onto the road.

Joshing who could chug-a-lug the most.

Jerked off several caps to make a jolly toast

...all's just swell.

If...

Juggling a bottle of gin while driving,

drinking,

smoking,

joking,

speeding,

gulping,

jawing.

Journey home won't take long.

Joke's on Dad ...didn't even know I was gone

all's going well.

all's well that ends well.

if...

Jalopy on my left is racing us.

Junction ahead; I'll pass him and the bus.

Justifying I'll be the real winner.

If...if?

47

Jumped the curb, crashed into a truck.

Jackass trucker,

as a driver he did suck,

but we ran out of luck.

Jammed against a concrete rail.

ablaze is my car's tail

slammed,

banged,

crushed,

smooshed

Juncture crash spilled flaring booze.

Jumped the curb afire.

Jettisoned a tire.

Jiu-jitsued and exploded, a dangerous condition.

All kids were burned beyond recognition.

Truck driver went home for dinner.

Just one question: who was the real winner?

Kaleidoscope

Kaleidoscope's imagery distorted your attention.

Knew you were wasted and wild...

                           behaving like a child.

Kick-started spending your pension.

Kept beers over-flowing to everyone.

Karaoke singers, kettle drummer, all having fun.

Keg-kindled intoxication causes your spending spree.

Kangaroos, you claim you saw, were also drinking free.

Kept insisting they're behind the bar.

Karma tonight, not in your wishing star.

Kind hearted you were, before you fell to the floor.

Kiss your drunken binge goodnight.

Knack of your being the king at the bar

Knocked out, unconscious past daylight.

Knucklehead... your drinking friends left.

Knew your money was gone before dawn.

Lassoed

Lassoed around your neck,

        tight as a hangman's noose.

Lariat rope tied this night,

        you'll never get loose.

Looped like a desperado

        corralled and headed for slaughter.

Liquor and drugs holding you in bondage.

Lucifer is your drunken name,

        your wicked deeds,

        played as a fatal game

        to satisfy your tyrannical needs.

        same as one insane.

Ligatures strung together into a knot

        below your gasping double chins,

        choking you for your horrific sins.

Lifeless life's blood drains to purgatory.

Left life labeled as a boozer...a user...a loser.

Lightning crashing in the sky,

        awakens me from a terrifying dream.

        I let out a horrific scream,

then I knew that I did not die.

Lesson of the nightmare I intend to heed.

Letting go of my addiction is what I need.

Labyrinth of drugs and weed,

> followed that passageway.

> Ambulated each day, going astray.

> Amok with my amigos,

> High flying like eagles.

> Some were alien illegals.

Living life sober and clean with no loophole,

> or slippery mishap to behold.

Lost in addiction no more.

Love of life not to ignore!

Love Lost

Love everlasting was our fervent wish,

Love launched by heaven from the very first kiss.

Levitating to rainbows above,

              we soared when we touched.

Living in celestial clouds where we embraced,

Legally we wedded for a lifetime of bliss.

Later... we lost ourselves

          In nightmares of drugs and alcohol.

Livelihood long gone now.

      Got hot wired,

         lazy,

            tired,

               then fired.

Laden with stacked up bills unpaid...

      like I care?

          now on Medicaid...

      little do I care!

Libido lost as well as my sober wife.

Lectures by her went unheard,

        my not hearing a word.

Left her with my endless excuses and lies

as my parting goodbye.

Label me ....a drunk,

I don't care!

Liquor and my stash is all I want in my life,

day and nite!

Liberating my thoughts to wonder,

whenever did the love leave?

Liquid thunder in my glass,

Load of weed in my pocket ass.

Lollygagging,

loitering,

littering,

longing,

lonely,

left alone.

Lament I have known.

Left behind the love of my past.

Loony-tunes and loathsome I've become,

Lethal addictions lure this bum,

Liaison with my bottle will forever last.

Mothers and Daughters

From life's seed, you and I intertwined.

> your life connected with mine,

> mine forevermore with yours.

From my womb

> god granted you your life,

> my dearest child.

From many tender months,

> you learned to crawl,

> when small.

> Then...

> with years

> to walk your pathway tall.

As your stature grew...

So did your kind and so loving heart!

The bond of mother and daughter

> still unites us forever more

> though the umbilical cord is severed.

Life's memories and struggles

> still, remain within our very core,

> still caring,

still sharing

joys,

sorrows

Dreaming of plans for our tomorrows.

You, my love, are the child I bore.

Decades ago upon my breast

You once sweetly sucked.

Now grown up

Showing the world your best

Alone you do soar!

Separate lives we pursued with the passage of time

as ought to be.

When you need me, I will be near,

to listen and hear.

To wipe away each tear.

Mother dear, I ignored the stories you did tell;

I used and boozed and spiraled down and fell

...to hell.

Life exposed me to its addiction test.

the experience became my obsession.

my soul became its possession.

The darkness was the sun eternally setting into the west.

Alone and apart I battled my own submission

into the raging furies of addiction.

Banishing substance abuse is a lifetime goal.

Fighting it with heart, body and soul!

I remembered our bonded knot,

blended tightly together,

so many years ago.

Braided strong, resolute, unyielding and unobstructable.

Yet each strand was free.

Mother, you taught me love and courage for

Me to be just me...

when I was young and sat upon your knee.

Drug free was what you taught me to be.

Yet, I tried cocaine and almost died.

My past memories I denied

of my childhood of real love and caring.

Rehab returned me to reality and sobriety.

Mother, thank you, for being you!

I love you so true!

ABC

56

Multiplication of Drinking

Minute amounts of alcohol first altering the heart:

the brain,

the body,

the psyche...

from the start.

Multiplying with another drink--then more

...more....more.

Merging to your inner core.

Madness and mayhem activated as you soar.

Most major and minor functions decrease.

Memory begins to cease.

Malignant disease of abuse claims another prey today.

Marathon of drinking unleashes a mesmerizing stay.

Memory loss from that first sip.

Manipulative excuses slurring from your lips.

Monologue always the same...

when you play your addiction game...

refuting,

denying,

lying,

maximizing,

57

micromanaging.

Moderation is past tense.

Miserable then overdosing makes no sense.

Magic of addiction claims another hangover...

Or will it be death today?

Narcotics

Narcotics numbs my senses and pain.

Necessary to tame my hurts and aches.

Nirvana blessed to keep me sane.

Nonstop prescriptions for my maintenance sake.

Needles injected camouflage, all 'til I wake.

Nurses give me a kiss of nighty-night.

Nausea comes and goes.

Nervous twitches touch my toes.

Numerous angels surround my bed

Nestled close, watching me from overhead.

Nice angels saying I'm only 3 years old.

Nightmare made me so icy cold.

Never before was I brave and bold.

Next they lift me upward to the sky.

No way thought I could really fly.

Now from high clouds, I wave goodbye

      from way...way from up above.

Now I'm forever in peace.

No more pain. It did cease!

Navigated by a white dove I did not die...

      for forever is love!!!

Obsession - Addiction: The Same

Obsession is nothing new:

>   booze, street drugs, or prescriptions used.

Often are abused or over-used too.

Odds are they created an "occupational hazard" for you.

Occasional use was your habit, just as an outlet.

Outgrew using from a little, to a lot.

>   Became nonstop.

Outline of an addict is an outcome of obsessions.

Overture overlapping to overkill.

Overnight you lost your will.

Only to get high on occasion is obstructed.

Oath now nil...

>   ...omen obtained your possessions and essences

>   ...opiates offered oppressive odious lessons.

Obviously a sign you've been chemically abducted.

Overpowered in both your body and mind.

Overcast shadows bind you all the time.

Occult oracle orbits you into an opaque subsistence.

Overpowered by an overseer despite your resistance.

Overdosed spirit will forever occupy nonexistence.

Pendulum

Pendulum of a foyer clock swaying...

perpetually forward...

then swinging backward...

tick-tock-tick-tock.

Pushing solemnly forward new seconds

beckons...

the presence of now,

never that moment to last,

thus ending the past.

Precious time has made a shadow cast.

Past ended,

descended,

cycling anew...

tick-tock-tick-tock

Past now forever through

lost

lapsed

gone

departed.

Phoenix is reborn when clean and sober.

Present day brings you a freedom of latitude.

61

Prestige comes as a prelude of grateful attitude.
Pride is restored

                    as an earned reward.

Program of A.A. recovery being read.
Proud to comply with what the "Big Book" said.
Payoff is to be clean and off the sauce.
Password was *honesty* toward myself and others.
Precious presents of sobriety were given to

                        first myself,

                        family and friends too,

                        my A.A. sisters and brothers,

                        and all others who saved my life.

Pathway's leading to my recovery anew.
Purgatory, prognostic pronounced, pulverized by proxy,

                        by my higher power.

Paved my way to abort substance abuse

                        each and every hour.

                        no more do I use.

Pledged to cherish living in the now.

                how?

Phrase is-*"Praise to life's deserved seconds."*

                so says the clock ticking still.

                Now you're well... not ill.

                Each day your willpower beckons,

through your higher powers.

Promising every hour passing with seconds,

tick-tock-tick-tock.

Prison Time: Chapter One of Two

Prison of your mind,

Held confined, doing your time

behind metal doors,

bars and razor wire.

Not at all sublime.

Walking in the line.

Just waiting out your time.

Part of you rages a war

behind those locked doors,

Persisting to stay in your past yesterdays.

Predicting, prophesying, and clinging to your old habits.

Proclaiming you can't do anything else but crime,

and serving your time.

Pacing and hating waiting for your release.

Penitentiary penalty period now is ceased.

Primary goal is get myself plastered and high.

Possibly a prostitute or two.

Pot too, before the day is thru.

Prison Time:
Chapter Two of Two

Partying all night long.

Pour me another.

Partaking puff after puff of my bong.

Prospect of breaking parole hanging over me.

Personality turns psycho with drugs and alcohol

Physically can't walk straight

>> when I'm tight

Pent up in the pen before

>> now just hanging out.

>> shouting and releasing it all.

>> having a great big ball.

Primal instincts surging, burning, bursting out.

Popped another drug, then two more.

>> am high and beginning to soar.

Pissed, I'm ready to start a war.

Provoked by another gang member,

>> but the rest...I don't remember.

Public defender lost my case.

Prison's where I will waste away.

Punishment is for life each and every day.

Put behind the metal door once more.

Past freedom is lost forevermore .

Pushover for that very first drug or drink

        addiction was in your core

        didn't you even think?

Promises vanished and banished.

Parents and family awaited your release.

Past tense... they know now to cease!

        labeled you as a loser

        drug user and boozer.

Proof was those metal bars clanging shut

        no ifs, ands, or buts.

Potential to reform was in a simple 12-step study.

Program of A.A. might have broken your addictions.

Parole lost, cause you just killed your buddy.

Quick Quiz

Question is, are you an addict?

to drugs?

to alcohol?

to meds?

Quick quiz--do you sincerely want to end using,

abusing,

boozing,

losing?

Quandary if life can be better, richer, fuller?

Quaff of overuse is not easy to stop, is granted.

Quest for answers ....

only you alone can be the judge

by stopping,

by withdrawing,

by no longer stalling,

by no more stonewalling.

Quality of your life is simply alone your choice.

Quintessence is enriched by a positive action decree.

Qualification for quitting is believing in you!

Question to answer... a clue.

Quantum jump sets you free

       hold on to being sober!

       let your past be over!

       trust only a true vision.

       it's your final decision.

       it's all up to you!

Quitting

Quota for your alcohol increases.

Quantity multiplies,

> drinking rarely ceases.

Quality of your life decreases.

Quick fix needed to function onward.

Quit really living long ago, so absurd!

Quenching your alcoholic thirst,

> always came first.

Question is when will you stop and curse?

Quest for a sober and clean life can begin.

Quandary of the need for more and more can end.

Qualifications are simple...

> just begin with the willingness to quit!

Qualms??? Questions???

Quick... toss out your rhinoshit!!!

Rainbows of Gray

Rainbows of your life were transformed to gray.

Ransomed you into an alcoholic today.

Rock bottom you hit:

> "on the rocks," is where you'll stay.

Review of your resume stated all is well.

Rhinoshit!

Reality reveals otherwise.

Reason--you're heading for hell!

Raving, you revolt and rebel.

Round the clock, you use.

Relinquish substance abuse to get well.

Renounce all, including booze.

Refuse recovery...then you'll lose.

Ritual of your façade...

> is a camouflage...

> a mirage.

>> This is what you tell and sell.

>> Drinking and using you hide so well!

>> Now, we'll play "show and tell."

Role of your polished exterior,

> begins to crumble.

Reunion with your bottle causes you to tumble.

Rewards of sobriety teach one to be humble.

Required, lest you do stumble.

Reposed face first onto mother earth.

Ripe now for recovery and your rebirth...

Remedy is based in self-honesty earned!

Radiant rainbows thenceforth are returned.

Restored to you is balance, lacking of vanity.

Replaced with resolve and sanity.

Relief is in recovery retained...

Remember all you once lost?

Countless was the cost to be regained.

Remission is a gift!

Remedy remains always void of any buts or ifs!

Reneging is the same.

Resurrection to sobriety isn't a game!

Retrogression by using again was insane!

Rigor mortis--only you're to blame.

Rite of passage failed as your final act!

Rainbows you hailed turned to solid black.

Reason of death...death of reason.

To sobriety you turned your back.

Sands of Time

Sand filtering through the upturned hourglass

Shifting their way pyramidally to a dune.

One grain of sand upon the other,

            each building one upon another.

Sands of your earthly time

Strained through alcohol and drugs, is running out.

            Entombed in glass, you are encaged.

Seconds turn into days

            then to years as you aged.

Sands funneling to the bottom of your glass cage

            caused by your addictive behavior,

            friendship with drugs and booze

            that in the end... you lose.

            Sober and clean would have been your savior,

            that you didn't choose.

Where will you be at life's end?

Comatose, dead, drunk, stoned--deceased?

Too late to feel life's beauty, that god had sent.

Chose instead, addiction's road is where you went.

Now at the bottom on your ass.

Motionless, encased in glass!

Life as you knew it has ceased.

Pivotal mutating, inverting, into in vitro life,

Sentenced and sequestered by substance abuse.

Now deprived of sensibilities, sensuousness suspended.

Temperance was never even tried or applied.

Yesterdays you lost being an abuser, boozer...loser

Today leaves you unable to feel forever!

Never to feel no more a whispering,

                whisking,

                        whirling,

                                swirling wind.

Nor a sandy shore

                to feel the sweep of the tide in surge or surf.

Never to feel bared feet

                with toes sinking into the coolness beneath

                while the August sun blazes above so warm.

Never to see frail, tiny, stubby fingers

                scoop out a tunnel to the sea

                or sculpt a pinnacle and ramparts to the sky.

Never to feel a breeze drifting upon a storm

                to rest at a mallard's nest.

Never to be blanketed upon a shore

                beneath a crescent moon

while lovers whisper between caresses and kisses.
Never to watch weathered, wrinkled, sun-bronzed hands

        pulling,

        tugging,

        lugging,

        finned fishes and prawns to shore.
Alcohol and drugs have trapped you in glass.
You're contained in crystalline forevermore.
Loved ones tried to save your ass.
Stayed stoned and drunk to your very core.
Your time is now buried

        under a pyramid of sepulchral sands.
Your demise plunged you to a sandy early grave:

        another unwise addict refusing to quit!

        otherwise, rejected recovery
Therefore--was a failure to save.
Paved your own way to your earthly grave.
Hourglass sands wet by tears

        turned into cement

        cosmos time is bent
Sealing you from future years.

Sons and Fathers

Dad, just want to say I love you.

but I can't respect you!

This is really hard to say...

but I don't want to be like you!

Being a drunk is not what I choose

nor a druggie.

Drinking and street and prescription pills,

turned you into a hard-core addict.

no way! Not for me!

I will stay away from you.

Drugs that would deprive me

of living my life with dignity and honor.

Please, see me as connected to the world, *not hiding,*

not escaping,

not distorting,

not diverting,

not cowarding

I want to grow up to be me!

not like you.

Blackouts are uncouth.

puking on yourself or...on the floor.

Nope...not for me.

My footprints, on this planet, will be stable and steady.

     not wobbling,

     not staggering,

     nor wavering,

     nor falling.

I want to grow up with courage and self-respect.

     sorry dad, I don't want to be like you!

I will muster strength to resist being like you.

     an alcoholic, a drug user...

     a loser and a boozer.

Dad again, I reach out my heart to you today.

     stop your drunken way.

     please, for your own sake and mine...

     quit for all of us who love you!

     but most of all, quit for yourself!

Change your compulsion and change your life,

You were not born that way.

Please, dad, don't die as a drunk and addict!

We all love you too much.

Allow us to know and respect you once again.

     Sincerely your,

     son

daughter

wife

father

mother

brother

sister

grandparents

aunts

uncles

cousins

friends

coworkers

neighbors

congregation

future grandchildren

and not to be forgotten-

the I.R.S.

P.S. Dad, we all want you to get and stay sober!

then I may grow up more like you;

to become a lot like the new you.

Sunrise

$\mathcal{D}$ arkness of night still blankets the morn.

Saved am I, from my addiction...now sober in life.

Night enshrouded in black velvet, disrobes...

Shimmering while dawn removes the shadows.

Soon will rise the morning's light.

Sunrise draws her rosy fingers, removing the night.

Awakening, she has yet to stretch and yawn.

Suddenly...bolts of rose, yellow and violet radiating,

streaming from her fingertips, creating dawn.

Sun gently ascending to become another day,

illuminating the sky.

Sobriety taught me to live, not to cry ...or die.

Sunshine spirited deep into my very being,

Streaming reality through both eyes to see.

Sprinklings of stardust as I stargaze.

Sober and not in a drunken or stoned stage,

each day is a new horizon for me.

Stimulating,

reinvigorating,

revitalizing,

Sweet sobriety as I age.

Talk and Walk

Talk a good talk...

But can you walk a steady walk?

Pathways won't all be downhill,

                    nor uphill...

There are detours and bends,

                              and dead ends.

Then there are cul-de-sacs that end.

Driving stoned or slushed, testing you...

                    or arresting you.

Did you not curb...

                    your substance abuse?

Or do you still use?

Stinking drunk as you cruise.

Under the drivers seat is your hidden booze.

Empty...that's not news.

Cans, bottles, or a flask...

Or is it pot or crack?

Doesn't matter what, you won't last.

Sipping,

nipping,

   slushing,

      gulping

On your homeward way.

Racing,

weaving,

speeding,

smashing,

crashing.

Breath positive for mucho liquor

Vomiting is foul and sicker.

Handcuffs or a ticket?

Walked the walk?

Talked the talk?

Slipped and fell off the wagon again?

will your benders ever end?

Bail denied.

Metal bars enclose you inside.

Neon-lit bars outside,

No more for you to slip and slide.

One to ten—may be your term.

Freedom from drugs you must learn!

To beat 'em, sobriety you must earn!

Unable

Unable to stop drinking or drugging?

Unending attempts vocalized,

verbalized,

tried to abide,

but you only cried and lied.

Unwilling to stay sober

Unbalanced; you're stressed and unstable.

addict is your label!

Unable to commit

rhinoshit!

you took another nip!

failed promises

of staying clean and sober

'til even one day is over.

Using and abusing again from the first sip,

once alcohol touched your lips.

whoops... again another slip.

Uncorked the bottle,

uncapped the pills,

plunged the syringe,

snorted the powder,

became unable in an hour

then took off on a binge!

hooked!

Unhinged,

unstrung,

untrustworthy

uncontrollable,

unaccountable,

undeniable,

unorthodox,

unappropriate,

unemployed!

Urge to escape to oblivion is overwhelming.

Unmitigated lack of control over yourself;

need an ultimatum.

Unified help by pros will guide you toward recovery!

Unfortunate. The other choice is...death.

Undertaker is all that's left.

Unless ...you give your last chance —*your very best!*

and nothing less!

Universal Ultimatums Unlocked

*U*mbilical cord once attached to mother and to mother earth

>>> and to the genetics of birth

>>>> for better or worse.

Unattached--lifeline was surgically cut away.

Uterus now empty; a child is born this day.

Undone: maternal physical attachment severed

>> Now left bare

>> Tiny lungs gasping for earthly air.

Uncharted pathway of the newborn yet...

>>>> uncertain,

>>>> unseen,

>>>> unknown,

>>>> undreamed.

Ultimately life's experiences and genes will shape the way.

Under mom and dad's loving... or indifferent care,

>>> whatever!!!

United by family's habits–good or bad–children learn.

Unguarded by neglect, then may follow:

>>> unhappiness,

>>> unhealthiness,

untruthfulness,

unscrupulousness

ungratefulness

Universal upbringing is somewhat the same,

With the same aim.

Uncounted years have past, your child has grown

Unshackled and loose now and on their own.

Umpteen uncontrollable vices may inflict hateful ways

Ulterior adult motives may enter the growing-up phase.

Undeveloped,

unnamed,

unexposed.

Addictions waiting for decades and days.

Unaware unceremoniously they uncoil and strike and bite

Unsuspectingly unprovoked spits out its poison, day or night.

Untrained to resist an asp's intoxicating kiss.

Unfailingly lowers to the serpents' hiss and kiss of death

Unconsciously caught in addictions' woven net.

Uncorked the intoxicating bottle,

Plunged the syringe,

swallowed the capsules

smoked the weed

Unbeknown where drugs will lead.

Unconsciously unsure what will occur.

Unpremeditated death for sure!

Unaware of substances' abusive lure.

Universal program of A.A. or rehab offered a cure.

Unmindful you were seriously ill.

Untreated unequivocally it will kill.

Underneath mother earth is your grave.

Undertaker's lid closes; you rejected aid to save.

Urges to use or drink usurped your unruly will.

Underground burial now where all is still!

Vino

Vino, a favorite of mine

               wine and more wine.

Vital before, during, and after I dine.

Velvet for my throat; goes well when I toke.

Vodka, vermouth, whiskeys, coke . . .ugh! Yuck!

Verdict is that I prefer wine to chug-a-lug.

Varying from white, to red, to rose.

Vintage varies each day.

Vowed not to be a lush.

            When drunk at myself I curse

                  needing to stop my drinking,

                  rethinking--then why am I sinking?

Vulgarities invade my thinking.

Vocalizing words not fit to be heard.

Vomiting like an erupting volcano.

Virus must be what I have;

           not something anal.

Victimized by a virulent flu.

               some kind that's new?

Vino? Did I overdo?

Violent puking all over the floor.

Very ill to my sore core.

Valid reason to try "A.A."

> their way.

Vainly cursing my invalid thirst.

Vamoose to detox

> and the Docs.

Validating all my kinds of signs.

Voicing out...I shout...*but I only drink wines!*

Woven in DNA

Woven into spirals, twirled and whirled.

Whisked my DNA threads in a twist.

Warp and woof bonded with a mother's kiss.

Woven was the tapestry of my world.

Warm to enfold my skin so bare.

Weave is intermingled by angel's care.

Weakness in the cloth is of my making.

Waking to temptations already there.

White is the color of my original birth cloth.

Willfully can I retain the purity? ... or ought...

        to use...

            to abuse...

              booze

                pot

                  drugs

Whenever drugs invite me by overtaking,

Witchcraft whispering wicked words...

        to use...

                  luring me,

              beckoning,

begging

mesmerizing.

Wizard challenges me to abuse my threads.

Whatever course I come to choose,

Will be my earthly cloak forevermore!

Whenever my genetic core is willfully tore.

X Marks the Spot

X marks the spot...

dot reveals liver is diseased,

seized by alcohol and substance abuse.

X-rays verify intensive damage

by your repeated use.

stoned, tipsy-reacting loose.

Facts are: you ignored that

loaned to you, was your life.

You flew higher than a kite

that last night.

Ending of your life is in sight.

Win or lose, oops ...you lost!

Sending notification to next of kin.

Ending wasn't just the liver,

cost of life was a large size overdose.

Too many drugs and alcoholic sauce.

Body struggled but lost.

X signed on the dotted line by doc for time of demise.

Humm...beautiful eyes!

Hope you were an organ donor!

Yes or No!

Yes... I can say to substance abuse.

Yeah, I also can yell out no way, too!

Yet, I don't have to give an excuse.

            A flat out "no" will do!

            That's my final word.

Yep, all else is absurd!

            Anyone else is a rhino turd!

Yesterdays

Of yesterdays when looking behind,

        capture only a fading glance.

Do not stare,

For when suspended in the past

Only shadows are cast.

Of today, grasp it, for it will not last.

Now use your granted time,

        bind your sobriety to today.

        To you it was awarded to stay.

        Choose your new sober pathway.

Inebriation and twisted hangovers are left behind.

Yielded

Yesterday of yore and before,

You saw me as a druggie and a drunk.

Yes, of course, a drug dealer.

   Naturally, a wheeler-dealer too.

Young yuppie that others feared and knew.

Yens of mine outsourced by my hired punks.

Yardsticks couldn't measure my piles of money.

Yakking near poolside lounged many a honey.

Yachts, yellow gold watches and dangling chains

   were mine.

Young women, by the dozen, I could claim.

Yielding to my every desire and wish –

Yellow golden blonde

   ruby red,

      velvet black

         hair colors of every kind.

Yesterdays of past I no more toed the line.

Yeah, I changed to law-abiding.

Yup, gave it all up, instead.

Yearned to be free of hiding.

of cheating,

of swindling,

of deceiving,

of hangovers,

of boozing,

of using,

of lying,

of my criminal past.

Yesterday wedded at long last

my love to be my wife.

along with my new life.

gonna be straight.

saint I ain't.

Ying and yang is my new style...

Yesteryear I was vile.

Yes! We said to the preacher with a smile.

Yielded and kneeled...

to love.

sealed with a promise

to the Man far up above.

Zonked Out

Zonked out on drugs again?

when will it end?

Zealous fanatic always high.

Zenith point in the sky to fly.

Zone in is lethal.

Zeitgeist is not legal.

Zest for drugs.

Zaps your body and mind.

Zero becomes your last sign in mankind!

Chapter 2

TOO MUCH

Appetite Addiction
And
Obesity

Appetite Addiction or Anorexia Nervosa?

*A*re you addicted to being *thin?*

slim?

skinny?

Answer - your scale reveals the real fact!

Anorexia nervosa shows weight loss,

of a major poundage lack.

Ate like a glutton,

afterwards,

into the toilet upheaving,

all of it you toss.

instant weight loss!

Anxious not to gain, is your every day aim.

Always have adverse fears to any gain

thus, puking to stay the same.

Asinine dieting to slenderness!

Annihilating all wellness.

Absent is healthy nourishment.

Annihilation just like a bulimic body

vomiting in the potty.

Anatomy's appearance is skin and bone

> muscles appear atrophic
>
> you lost all muscle tone
>
> gorging or eating like a bird.

Adding alcohol the calories will upward surge as you splurge.

Again and again repeatedly occurs the urge to purge.

Advice: take control of your malnourishment;

Accept healthcare as your daily mission.

Addiction dwells in your mind

Add in self-encouragement

Allow yourself to cherish your life's time.

Also stop self-abuse and alcohol use.

Audit and alleviate your pain

Authorize medically your eating plan.

Agree with an alignment you accept.

Absolution is a given sign

Always to yourself be kind:

> heed the bottom line
>
> to diet as a healthy winner
>
> while becoming thinner.

Brother's and Sister's Reunion Blast

Brother's and sister's reunion at last.

Bet it's gonna be a blast!

Boy, sis has gained a ton of weight.

Barrel-size now from whatever she ate.

Built curvaceously in past, years ago.

But blubber fat on sis had its tow,

    ya know...

Brief me in, what's new?

Bariatric surgery you plan to pursue?

        great plan for you!

Brooklyn hospital is where you'll go?

Banish all that weight from all you ate!

        it's not too late!

Bluntly said ....think you are too tubby,

        like your hubby.

Bro...what's new with you?

Bigger than ever...rhinoshit--you too!

Brawny muscles gone that bulged each summer.

Believe you're also a tonner. What a bummer!

Beer belly is blown out to outer space.

Bet ya get bonus buys on sale by the case.

Back to our talk after dinner

Beseeching you again to be a winner.

Bottom line is you're a boozer.

Binge-brew and buffet-food user.

Bourbon was to quench your thirst.

But besotted and bizarre behavior...

        tonight you got worse!

Blackout came first.

Body's breakdown urgent.

Blood pressure soared sky high.

        too late for a surgeon!

Because... who knows why???

Blame it on self-abuse for a fact.

        he was so young to die!

Bleak outcome from a massive heart attack.

Bereavement and a hearse

        to the burial site.

Before I fly away in morn's first light,

        mourning on my homeward flight.

But, my diet will start <u>tonight</u>!!!

Certified Fatso

Certifiable fatso you allowed yourself to become!

Challenge to exercise and diet you refused.

Custom to eating a lot nonstop and abused.

Cakes and candies and goodies you bought.

Cutting calories curtailed...but not stopped.

    now in cyberspace.

Crusade for recruiting me is a waste!

Constantly crave food yummy to my taste.

Creature of excess eating is my pleasure.

Creed of mine is to gorge at my leisure.

Cumulative pounds I just don't measure.

Convert to counting calories--screw you!

Can't have you control what I ingest...

Criticism and your tape measure test.

      Just go away.

Customarily I crave many foods every day.

Cuisine cooked in every way.

Crazy about creamy cupcakes.

Crisp fried chicken too, I ate.

Choice is chocolate and champagne to celebrate.

Cessation of my favorite foods, no chance.

Calculation continuously of what I ate

Calisthenics...exercises am never in the mood.

Counting calories campaign... No way!

Cancel me out today, tomorrow and any other day.

Consume whatever I like!

Crystal clear?

        Not wanting to be mean... but

                take a hike!

        Get out of my sight!

Comfortable here,

With my fried chicken and beer.

        You and your scale go disappear!

Children and Food

Children's compulsion of over-eating, a plague!

Copycatting mother, father or some other?

Consuming junk food and rarely healthy cuisine.

Corpulent condition makes one want to vomit or gag.

Crusade of weight control also needed for mother,

because her body layers do sag.

Cradle to crawling,

to walking,

to talking,

to a preteen,

Countless calories resulted in a fatty body...not lean.

Considered medically unhealthy!

Color that dangerous fat "red" this time.

Consider it as a danger sign.

Cut out fatty, sugary, and greasy food.

Crash eating when in a bad mood?

Control your food portions

and your emotions.

Can't lose that fat in a dream night!

Constrain yourself at a flashing red light.

Confront it as a signal not to take a bite.

Conquer overweight as a life fight.

Confidence in yourself can and will win.

Compete 'til you're a "fatso has-been!"

Closure ongoing after you're healthy and thin.

Coronary

Convalescing from a coronary last year...

Cardiologist confronted me to diet.

        nope, no hope, I won't buy it.

          Nor try it.

Cessation of my cannabis was included, too.

Cabernet sauvignon, all liquor and beer was barred

Confession is I just don't care if I'm a tub of lard

Compulsory

        customary

        continuous

          consumption

          consuming

           cooking

Cramming down culinary treats I love to eat.

Can't be beat!

Categorically I state...no diet!

Cardiac arrest the coroner claimed.

Catalyst casualty of obesity was also the blame.

Coincidentally, the family's ashamed of being the same.

Conversation about the cost of an extra wide coffin.

Casket custom-made for the cadaver's huge size.

Cost too dearly for a double wide.

Cremation was cheaper those days.

Cemetery crypt is now where fatty lays.

Dirty Word

*D*iet!!!

Dirty word to those diagnosed as obese.

Doctor said to downsize!

Develop new eating habits, get wise!

Death and diseases are no surprise.

Developed by being overweight equals early demise.

Discouraged with dieting before, of course

   for you kept eating like a horse.

Digested appetizers, seconds of the main course.

Double desserts equaled double digits on the scale.

Deduct that blubber or look like a beached whale.

Detoxify that pile of junk food garbage you eat.

Death comes earlier if it is a medical prognosis.

Defeat your layers of fat with action and courage.

Disparage not, just visualize shedding pounds...

   diminishing...

      disappearing...

         disgorging...

            dissolved

               dwindled

Disorder of overstuffing is conquered at last.

Diabetes gone too, along with the fat ass.

Diligent healthy eating in earnestness...

　　　now the patient weighs far less.

Decimals on the scale surpassed the test.

Deep-sixed many pounds away.

Death lurks if one gains again that way.

Elevator Eating

Empowering you to lose weight is my intent.

Enemy is yourself/no one else.

Enlightenment to you sent.

Excessive eating no more.

   for...

Elevators can stop at any floor.

Exit or go up and down.

	Down	and	up.
	Down	and	up.
	Down	and	up.
	Down and up.

Elevator eating, losing ne'er a pound

Evasive excuses of gorging more.

Endless denial is just plain lying .

   Obesity sooner results in dying.

Embalming follows life's ending.

   OR...

Embrace fat elimination, called a diet war.

Emphasize patience, just try it.

   like a garden is weeded;

again and again as needed.

bore into its core.

Elephantine body elegantly reshaping...

Enormous size descending

slipping away

surplus fat lost each day

spiraling downward.

Exiled to a basement floor,

as garbage in a pile it will stay.

Extinction of those extra pounds is up to you.

Express elevated eating ensued is no more.

Epitaph and eulogy unwritten for now

erstwhile was a fat cow.

Emerged in euphoria

Enumerate the number you lost.

not needed.

Eliminated... now gone.

Empowerment in life you've achieved!

Food Fiesta

Field day of food and fun

Festivity under the sun

Frankfurters on a mustard bun.

Fried fruit fritter cakes

Frosted donuts and fast food

Fancy-free is my mood.

Feast not famish is my intent.

Fantasizing frozen icicles in the big tent.

Fudge candy by the squares

Feeding my face without cares.

Fantastic family day

Flat out don't care what I weigh.

Fast forward--now I'm as big as a whale.

Forgot I have an unforgiving scale!

Faults of mine include frenzies of overeating.

Facing a sudden freak out I'm not needing!

Future health fringes on a serious diet!

Fact is to live longer I have to do it.

                    Shit!

Gigantic Farts

*G*obbling,

    guzzling,

       gulping,

          gorging,

Girth growing wider.

Girdle getting tighter.

Gigantic ass!

Gusty farts due to overloaded gas.

Gross smells when they pass.

Gorged food all day.

        What else can one expect?

Gushers of farts bombarded out.

Goodbye, guests shout.

       We won't stay.

       No way!

Gasping for clean air,

Guess you know the sign.

Granted... their comments are not kind.

Gusto for stuffing food was your pastime,

          then you crossed the line

            eating all day and night.

Gravity of your blubber is not a healthy sight.

Glutted down food with every bite.

Gigantic body size in xx extra large is a disgrace.

Gastronomy is food of healthy good taste.

                      not just to increase your waist.

Gluttons choose that no food goes to waste.

Greedy one gratifying your body and chubby tubby face!

Grateful you're not...*yet*... in a graveyard?

Gutless to diet and became a fat tub of lard.

Gravestone, where gray clouds loom,

                 is your tomb.

                        soon, soon.

Gripe and groan about this poem.

Grumble, mumble, but you're still jumbo

                  as well known.

Gruesome fact is you refused to diet.

Giant farts are expelled each day.

Guaranteed that with gumption,

            not just an assumption,

              those fat globs will go away!

Got no willpower so you ate and ate.

Gambled with your weight.

           Alas it's too late!

Gourmand obsession buried you one grim day.

Gossip is... ghost farts haunt your tomb.

Gruesome smells if exhumed!

Holidays and Celebrations

Holidays bring joyful spirits

       especially when poured from a bottle.

       spirited drinks for the inner spirit.

Hallelujah for celebrations throughout the year

Host and hostess with trays of alcohol and beer.

Hors d'oeuvres on a silver platter

         just can't resist!

Hootenanny singers and swayers on the main floor;

Humorous laughter howling near the door.

Hurrah for parties like this!

Hurry and give all a kiss.

Hoedown begins later.

Hunger attacking,

          stomach reacting,

        growling,

         grumbling,

          rumbling.

Hesitate to gulp down some highballs

Hooked on food, so called to the waiter.

Happen to be salivating for food first;

         eating comes before thirst.

Happy hour can come later.

Highlight is the food laden table.

Hypnotized by homemade food and haute cuisine.

Happen to be stout; not thin and beanpole lean.

Hospitality deserves a high-five!

Hallelujah! Hosanna! Hurray!

Hell bent to eat all I'm able today.

Heavenward soon I'll go unless I stop.

Heaped full my plate to overflow,

                              up over the top.

Hoggish of me I know too well.

Habit next, is to get high or drunk as hell.

Hung over and not feeling well.

Hanky-panky sex is nix.

                    am needing a fix.

Heinous hallucinations is a hapless fate.

Horrific heart pain did not wait!

Harm caused, now too late!

Headstone on a six by six

                due to his obese weight,

                'cause of all he had ate!

Huge Hog

Heavy is too huge to lift that poundage, honey.

Humongous husband over qualifies too, sonny.

Hoist aloft a crane, or a pulley is needed.

Hogged down food hunks plate after plate.

Hunger sated, still you ate and ate.

Heart failure on its way.

Habitual bloating with weight gain

Hazardous to your health.

Hedonism you'll pay for some soon day.

Headstone engraved where you lay.

Inauguration of Weight Loss

Inauguration begins inside your head.

Intention is to not "pig out" instead.

Inches will decrease as you become more mobile.

Impact on your blubber image starts to shrink.

Instigated diet and exercise as your weight loss link,

In interim you gain pride and feel noble.

Interior and exterior of your mind and body freer.

Inhibition against excessive food and beer.

Irrefutable you are becoming slimmer,

                              thinner

                                 a real winner.

Irresistible urge to diet became your victory now!

Irresistible beauty you became.

Insensible eating was the blame.

Inalienable courage to remain slim and sane.

Jumbo Size

Jaw opens wide,

Jamming your food inside.

Journeyed down to your big tummy

Junk food you declare to be so yummy.

Justifying your mounds of jiggling fat

Jaded from eating all that.

Jam-packed food gulped down

Joining several more than a mere pound

Jiggle yourself around to hear a noisy sound.

Just is your tummy's digestive track...

                                        cursing you back.

Judge for yourself!!!

Judgment should be of your health!

Kids and Obesity

Kiddies nowadays are roly-poly tubbies

              so very round chubbies.

Kept on growing bigger outward

       one would say, is absurd!

Kinfolk also likely to be fatties

Know its mommies and daddies.

King and queen-sized one would assume

Kitchen is family's favorite room.

Kinds of fatty foods there to consume.

Kaput goes a healthy lifestyle!

Keep it up . . . 'til early death will be no denial!

Large or Obese

Large or is the fitting word obese?

Lover of food eating seems never to cease

Legitimately obese wins its alphabet place.

Larger or largest is the sizing case.

Layered love handles at the waist.

Lopsided body loins wiggle and swish.

Liverwurst loaded in a dish, calorie free you wish.

Loaves of bread share with lobsters a full plate.

Linguine or lasagna unlimited you ate.

Lunch you munched all you could eat.

Landed by spreading across your backseat.

Leftovers gobbled down not to waste.

Lavishing every bite to taste.

Lessons of health you didn't learn.

Loosey-goosey attitude without concern.

Lumbar spine is sagging due to overweight.

Lethal diseases, diabetes, heart problems too.

Leaking gross smelly farts are nothing new.

Likelihood your lifeline's shorter.

Listen to Doc's order.

Lose that weight!

Lurking death doesn't wait!

Mouthful

Mouthwatering goodies to swallow.

Mood foods along with a beer bottle.

Moderation not practiced here.

Minimal amounts not even for beer.

Massive bodies when mobile, do waddle.

Mammoth fat asses seated near.

Medical miscellaneous problems follow.

Misfortunes of obesity made crystal clear.

Most unmotivated tubbies turn a deaf ear.

Multiplying,

      adding,

            accumulating.

Myriad of pounds gained each year.

Morgue has an open invitation.

Most of all for those obese in the nation.

Mourners can languish a monsoon cry.

Morning,

   noon,

     or night,

       to those who did die.

Naked

Nude dude - nude dame

Needed to play this game.

Not naughty or nice

Nor gamblers with dice.

Neanderthals unthawed

Nonpartisan who's declawed.

Neurotic or a psychotic

Novice or a nincompoop

No one's left out of my soup!!!

Nobility or numskulls in the loop.

Non-alcoholics or loser boozers

Nymphs driving red cruisers

Nobody's denied my soup bowl.

Number of calories, please be low.

Never take huge portions to eat;

Naturally overeating ends in defeat.

Naked--now look in a looking glass mirror.

Nanoseconds later you will see why:

Noxious fat from head to toe, ear to ear.

Number of calories you did gain;

      is the name of the game.

      Your greedy mouth is to blame!!!

Ounces Add to Pounds

Ounces, pounds, form your body.

Once you were slim and trim.

Only now you're a bundle of bulging fat.

Obese from--eating,

        stuffing,

          gorging,

            shoveling downward...

Obscene tons of food.

            How absurd is the abuse of yourself.

            No consideration of your health.

Outcome likely to be diseases of the heart.

              Pile that in your shopping cart!

Over in the next aisle is *diabetes*.

            That goes in the cart, too.

            Also add regular medical problems anew:

            clogged arteries, lung congestion

            in the cart,

            add *your liver*, as well.

            Time will tell what else.

            Fatso, you're not well!

Overweight because of all you ate.

Opinion is stop the orgies, death does not wait.

Otherwise diet has to change before it's too late.

Overcome your eating compulsion and lose weight.

Obstacle of obesity, in your way is *only you!*

Overdosing on food becomes self-hate.

Courage to conquer your obsession, in your case.

Objective is to avoid *your obituary*...just don't hesitate!

or wait!

Puking

Pounds put on are not easily lost.

Pampered your cravings for food,

        whenever you're in the mood.

Purgatory ounces gained also count and cost.

Purging is like pus pumping out a putrid smell.

Puzzled why you look like hell?

Punishing your body, well... do tell.

Pungent odor, smelling as a stinker.

Puking up your guts has a proclivity to linger.

Projectile vomit is often a bulimia case.

Predator of your own body going to waste.

Plain and simple, you threw up what you ate.

Planned to be a penthouse pinup by losing weight.

Penalties to your internal organs cost your health.

Paparazzi didn't bring you wealth.

Paramedic was your life savior.

Problem was an eating disorder behavior.

Patient promised to purge no more.

Prognosis is most favorable.

Psychiatric care to explore your inner core.

Put it on your list.

Promise yourself that, I insist!

Queen and King-Size

Qualified my going from fat to thin.

Quit devouring food as fatty as sin.

    game of weight loss I intend to win!

Quantity reduced and so did I.

Quality outranked fast greasy food.

Quest for low calorie

    meant carrots and celery

Queen or king-size portions before I ate!

    made me overweight.

Quaffed down beer, wine, and chocolate shakes.

Quarts, I say, not a teenyweeny dainty glass

    proof was I had a fattso ass,

    looked like an overgrown melon.

Quenched my thirst even by the gallon.

Quibbled how I ate to become a fat pig.

Question is...yea, then I ate the whole cake.

Quandary erased now for I'm wide awake.

Quit my addiction now and won't renege!

Reduction

Reflection resembles a small rhino.

Relative to your size or a baby dino.

Reduction of massive poundage a project

Realize to dieting you might object.

Rumor has it you once tried.

Rollercoaster diet, how you lied.

Raided the fridge, day and night.

Ravenous appetite gulped all goodies in sight.

Ridiculous gorging of all you ate.

Rich caloric foods added pounds and weight.

Reality is your obesity destroys your health.

Regurgitating food is harming yourself.

Rest assured a doctor will guide you how.

Rehabilitation loses looking as a fatted cow.

Regimen of diet and exercise slenderizes.

Ravishing look now, without xx-large sizes.

Scales Don't Lie

Scales tipping with pounds moving ...

climbing upward.

downward... never...ever.

Spinning dial zooming up...up...up

upward toward the absurd.

Stuffed your tummy full again today.

Sorry, to say, but you're obese!

Sympathy, you won't get from others,

not a truthful word at least.

Scales don't lie!

Sanctuary is your gulping down more food.

Scenario--reality is look in a mirror--totally nude.

Scan yourself, front, sideways, and backside.

Super-duper size you can't hide,

for mirrors don't lie.

Sabotaging, self-destructing, binge feeding.

Seduced by overeating.

Seldom refusing helpings of a second or third.

Spoonfuls – whoops! – that shovel on the side.

Safeguard health by stopping the urge.

Self-restrained with a scale to abide.

Teeny-Weeny Bitsy

Teeny-weeny bitsy is no longer me.

Technically I'm called obese now

    or even a fat sow

        or cow.

Topsy-turvy I've become.

Transformed into a tubby

Tummy overlapping with folds.

Thought of getting a tummy tuck...

Tape measure numbers give me dismal displeasure.

Tyrannosaur and I must have akin genes.

Truth is I feel I weigh a ton.

Tranquility for me is eating time...

    how sublime when I dine

    and drinking nine glasses of wine.

Time to turn off the overeating button and diet.

    overweight and can't deny it.

Tombstone time creeping near; so no more shit!

Toking,

    smoking,

        drugging,

guzzling booze are out!

Time to live life thin and trim.

Tabulate all the lost pounds after I win!

Under or Overweight

Undersized or oversized, which are you?

Unalike are the two.

Unable to walk without wobbling?

Ungracefully shifting from side to side,

                  left to right,

                  fat you can't hide.

Unstable movements in whatever you do.

Unhealthy a sight!

                  nothing's new about you.

Understand it's your baggage of extra weight

                  from the food you ate.

Unless you shed those calories the pounds will remain.

                    ain't you ashamed?

                    only you're to blame!

Under your clothes, the fat wiggles up and down

                    and all around...

Ungracefully shifting...

          drifting,

          jiggling,

              bouncing up and down.

pound after pound... you're overweight!!!

Unhealthy and insane.

Underestimating you're playing a death-defying game!

Understand you have to diet before it's too late.

Unlucky if you delay, for death doesn't wait!

only you'll be the blame!

Victim of Bulimia

Victim of vanity!

Vogue is to be lean and thin.

Volunteer of insanity.

Vice of bulimia propositions you to be slim.

Voracious pattern of overeating binge.

Very bile

        vile

          violent

            vomiting

                above the commode you bend.

Various varied chunks and vital liquids puked out.

Vitamins lost too.

Vanishing weight destroys your body insides.

Voiding 'til your stomachs contents is... emptied,

        heaved out,

           ejected,

              upchucked.

Vicious cycle of urges of eating ...then of purging,

Violation of your body,

Verified facts by the medical field.

Value your life by losing your strife.

Vanquish your potty venture.

Vamoose to a healthy body adventure.

Victory

Vow what weight do you choose to be at?

Vertical and slim and thin?

Versus horizontal and bulging with fat?

Vice you're addicted to is overfeeding your face.

Volumes you taste, nothing goes to waste.

Valuable nutrition not to your taste.

Vegetables are infrequently on your plate.

Various sweets and carbohydrates you ate.

Vending machines you can't pass by.

        Coins go in for the junk food you buy.

Verdict is you spread sideways more and more.

Vast amounts of food ingested then upward pounds soar.

Value of those calories are nil, just pure sugar.

Verdict is there's more vitamins in your nasal booger.

Vice of yours is an addiction of overeating.

Void of the valid nutrition your body is needing.

Victim of voluminous buttocks.

Vital signs are in a dangerous zone.

        Flab is not muscle tone.

Various health issues are already known.

more will be lurking,

invading your body.

Victory of your life is conquer your weight!

Veto fatass foods before it's too late.

Vitality is empowered by pounds shed

Victorious view the mirror reflected.

Valid is the scale.

Verified a voluptuous you

Versus a voracious whale.

Vision of you reviewed as in vogue.

Video playback of haute couture

Vindictive pay back won

Vanquished are all those

vile,

vast,

fatass tons.

Vaporized those voluminous buns.

Weigh in Time

Weigh in time!

Waddle to the scale.

Are you looking like a whale?

Wait... let me tell you a tale.

When the numbers rise higher and higher.

What can you expect?

Your scale is not a liar!

Wider you become when more pounds are acquired.

Waistband stretching isn't something you desired.

Waiting for a miracle? Nope, no easy way!

Dieting is the price you have to pay.

What about starting today?

Want those pounds to go or stay away?

Which way?

Whatever... it's up to only you.

Whisk those ounces off, pounds will follow.

Willpower will improve in each tomorrow.

Workouts will strengthen your body's core.

Wonderful way to lose more and more.

Wage a winning fatso war...

or keep on the fatty food chain...

and pounds are gained,

adding layers of blubber.

Whatever!

Will winning be your endeavor?

XXL

XL - stands for extra large size.

XXL is bigger yet.

Fat can't be disguised

or be denied!

It shows from head to toes

in any clothes,

everybody knows.

Plumpness is mountains of pounds.

Stoutness is just as it sounds.

Overweight? Your health you're losing

more if you're boozing.

Pick a diet of your choosing.

Stick to it and blubber will melt every day.

Finally, it will pay off, when fat stays away.

Or you can still wear X's, and weigh a ton.

Or if you care enough, diet, be tough!

Become a slim beauty, even in the buff.

Fight the battle of the bulge.

Don't overindulge!

Until you've won

showing off your tan under the sun.

Yo-Yo Diets

Year after year you swore to diet.

You don't deny it.

Yet you just ate and ate.

Yo-yo diets when you lost, then gained weight.

Yummy food for your tummy!

Yoga you tried and exercises.

Yardstick showed you got fatter.

Your curves are displaced by blubber.

Youthfulness now ballooned to oversized.

Your mouth gulps down food, food, food.

Yet it matters not, whatever your mood.

Yesterday you overdid it again.

Yummy yummy for a fatter tummy

your legs and thighs,

your flabby arms,

your wobbly ass.

Yuck, yuck, no luck.

Yummy Foods for All my Moods

Yesterdays ago I weighed just right.

  in skintight dresses I was a sexy sight.

Young yuppie moving up the corporate ladder

  skipping meals never did matter.

   when retired I just ate and ate.

   on and on... 'til I was sate.

Year after year, pounds I easily gained.

  my appetite couldn't be tamed.

Yielded to tasty temptations.

Yo-yoed diets after vacations

  up and down

  got fat all around.

Yule time ...yikes all those invitations!

  ate all chef-inspired sensations.

Yellow to try a diet?

  yeah...I can't deny it.

Yearned for kinds of creamy dreamy cake

  ate them all, for my psyche sake

Yummy things for my tummy

  yum-de-yum, yummy!

Zits

Zits peppering on your frowning face.

Penalty for sugary desserts you ate.

Don't forget all the greasy foods

gobbled up to calm your moods.

Every yummy one you did taste -

none did you waste.

Zinger is: fat also settled on your waist.

Chapter 3

Gambling

Ante Up

Ante up time.

Aphrodisiac, adrenaline create an awesome high.

Add alcohol to amplify my flying to the sky.

Addiction is undeniable, so no need to analyze why.

Auspiciously assembling my cards neatly in a line.

Aspiring attitude; assuring me of a lucky sign.

Anticipating I'll win, with aces high I can't lose.

Already I'm celebrating with more booze,

Assumed wrong!

A royal flush won the poker game at end.

Aftermath is adversity, I'm broke again.

Affirmative! I'll be back,

      with cash, for another stack.

Agenda is to win an amazing massive amount.

      and gain yesterday's loss back.

Anxious for another attack.

      at another winning whack.

Another day I'll be back in a win-win act.

Black Magic

Bummer! Lost all my chips in roulette.

Boogied over to a card table to bet.

Bloody Mary in my shaking hand,

      sat down next to a bomb-shell blonde

Blushed and smiled. Just hope she has a magic wand.

Bought my chips and anted in.

Bluff with my cards, and hope to win.

Body language of the beauty infers sin.

Blood shot eyes fixated as I stare

      bewitched by her golden hair.

Bikini or on a bear skin rug totally bare.

Biorhythm gone crazy.

Blood pressure must be high.

Blinded by her, forgot to check out my cards.

Bankruptcy for me, if I lose.

Better order more booze.

Black magic baby come to me.

Black jack aces to build up my cash.

Black magic honey bewitching me.

Busted my budget as well as my ass.

Broke to the bottom line.

Bookmaker says, "Here, just sign!"

Blonde beauty hustled away.

Blundered once, but not the next day!

Casino Blues

Casino fever I possess!

Card skills put to a test.

Climax is winning more, not less.

Coins placed in the slot.

Casualty of gambling addiction.

Control lost like a feverish infection.

Closing in on a big time win.

Close, but lost to the machine of tin.

Cluelessly,

      curiously,

            capriciously.

Calculations refigured once again.

Compulsion costly at the day's end.

Charged more and more to the credit card.

Cards captivated the next win

          as sure as sin.

Certainly considerable cash would be won.

Challenge was a catastrophe--lost all, won none.

Chronic gambler will return.

Clenching a wad of bills--"money to be burned."

Casino consumed all the cash I earned.

Confirmed I haven't yet learned!

Derby Day

Post time, horses out of the paddock,

           panting,

              prancing,

               parading,

Heading for starting line.

Jockeys mounting on top their steeds

                      nearing race time.

Soon they will stampede...

        each ready to take the lead.

Horses protest entering the starting stall.

Jockeys urging unwilling haunches

          into the cage.

Countdown begins for the final call.

Wagers have been made.

An oval track becomes the stage,

       and they're off...

Front-runner is far aloof.

Favorite's wedged next to the rail.

One broke loose from the back pack

         she begins her horse's attack

accelerating

straining,

gaining,

advancing.

Jockey speeding on her steed;

he took the lead.

Now in the stretch... the greatest test.

Crossed the finish line to beat the rest.

Hurrahs and shouts of glee filled the air.

Single rose placed into jockey's long hair.

Garland of roses around horse's neck.

She and he proved to be the best.

Triple crown is next!

Extracurricular Extravagance

Establishment that electrifies me is a casino.

Elaborate or casual, I don't care.

Eatery there that also serves Italian vino.

Easy to forget my recent chemo.

Easier to forget things I can't bear.

Earmarked cash I spin away.

Eliminates my despair.

Eloquently I say, I just don't care.

Earth won't be my home much longer.

Elevated to a higher place I'll wander.

Emotions calm as I ponder.

Enraptured now with gambling and fun.

Extracurricular games above are won.

Extraterrestrials told me so in my dream.

Ending is only a beginning, so it will seem.

Fanatic

Formulated methods to win at a poker game.

First checked facial expressions of players.

Fuddy-duddies tend to play slow and tame.

Frustrated ones shed emotions in layers.

Friendly ones yell and cuss.

Found those guys not to trust.

Failure to miss a fault today--I lose.

Finding it best not to play and booze.

Flush in my hands, I bet all I can.

Forced to forfeit or bet to the end.

Flat-out lost to a fetching blonde.

Fast forward to my loss thereafter on

Found fault with my fallacy in my game.

Fabricated a new formula not the same.

Four-flusher gal, go to hell.

Former theory didn't sell.

Fresh start, new way today.

                Furthermore ...

Feel jackpot heading my way.

Gambling

Gambling's a losing addiction.

Gap between reality and fiction.

Goal is to win lots and lots.

Good luck at the tables or slots...

Greed, a motive here.

Guzzling down gin or beer.

Glutton for punishment.

Guessing I'm just hell-bent.

Gigantic jackpot was an astonishment.

Gratitude for my win...a blessing sent!

               with a promise to recall Lent.

Horse Racing, an Addiction

Horses mounted ready...

for the trumpeters calls

saddles tight; jockeys all ready

entering starting metal stalls.

Horseback riders ready for their mount's flight.

Lined up at the start for a fight.

Bets placed—win, show or place.

Tickets clutched in both my hands

waiting seated in the stands.

Do I hold a winner...an ace?

gun shot blast...

sending the panting beauties into motion.

Handicapper predictions were past cast.

Hapless before trying to control my emotion.

Hearing, seeing four hoofs,

flying,

speeding,

competing,

weaving,

recouping.

Horses galloping down the track

around the oval bend.

My steed is in the pack,

but way too far back

jammed in too close to the rail.

Got no way to close the mounting gap.

Jockeys round the final lap.

Hearts and hoofs pounding.

Horses panting.

sweat pouring.

crowds standing,

screaming,

shouting.

now the final stretch,

finish line in sight.

My favorite's not even placing,

barely crossing.

again another day at the races!

bet all! Lost all!

be back another day

I say...

another horse

another call

Hope my luck takes a better course.

Impulsive

Intentions are to multiply, not subtract.

Intuition internalized, this is my lucky time.

Invincible act of winning; I will not lack.

Inventory of chips will upward climb.

Instinct of mine tells me to attack.

Invisible entity covers my back.

Inalienable impressions are on my side.

Impossible to lose with an imported guide.

Imagination reveals a money landslide.

Idiosyncrasy of mine is an implanted sign.

Intoxicated... no way, with liquor or wine.

Impervious to implements of any kind.

Influx of income, a gift from a celestial.

Inspiration is impulsive-inspired instinct.

Influence of my alien is irrevocably inferential.

Iron clad is our irreversible link.

Impulsive gambling is in my nature.

Intermission over-- time to bet my wager.

Jackpot

"Joie de vivre" joy of life...mine is to gamble.

Jaunty attitude at the casino as I amble.

Jackpot, I pray, awaiting me!

Just going to win, you'll see.

Jubilation day will be a jamboree.

Jacks, kings and queens will be the key.

Jazzy outlook as I play.

Jaded no more today.

Jinxed no longer is my outlook.

Junky cards not dealt or took.

Jacks and royals in my hand

Jittery as the dealer shows his...and

Jolted to see his aces in a row.

Jealous jackass, admittedly, I know.

Jugular struck high and below.

Jigger juiced at the bar.

Jalopy, not a Jaguar, is my car.

Jaunt onward to home, not far.

Jai alai tonight, maybe I couyld.

Just maybe next day a horse race.

Jockey's "tip" could be good.

umm... tomorrow I'll see?

Karma

Karma has left me stranded.

Keno I played left me empty handed.

Knuckleheaded me played game after game.

Kindled fire made me bet higher.

Keen on betting more of the same.

Kept on losing.

    began boozing.

Kaput today.

Knocked out with a hangover tonight.

Kick-start 'morrow...

    by betting at dawn's first light.

Lottery

Luck is not in our control.

Lotto plays are purchased.

Lumberjacks, ladies, lawyers,

Loony-tunes, lieutenants, lovers

Logic-users, others and mothers

Lots of people play and pray.

List of those obsessed grows everyday.

Loyal to their chosen numbers

Low or high others dreamt in slumbers.

Lady luck spins the balls.

Long shots often are calls.

Looming on a winner's page,

Lining up players of every age.

Laughing nearby is their sage.

Magic Money

Magic of gambling knows no moderations.

Monomania morphine-like sensations,

                         emotions,

                         stimulations.

Mesmerized by the cards in my hand.

Minimum bet was my plan.

Miraculous *four gold aces* bold.

Mediocre I averaged before.

Mystified why I never did score.

Mismatched cards had grown so old.

Magnitude mostly of ante cash load

Maintain my composure, make it last.

Magic before that I've never known.

Moderate my words and tone.

Motivate the other players to bet is my task.

My mission is to get the bets higher.

My morale broken … they all folded and retired.

Numbers and Symbols

Necessary to have coins to machine feed

Numbers and symbols wins fulfill a need.

Nickname for slots is big-time "coin guzzler".

Nickels, quarters swallowed by the hustler.

Nitty-gritty – it's a non-profit situation.

Notorious reputation ruining a vacation.

Nouveau riche for moments, then taken away

Nothing gained, everything lost ever day.

    nonproductive

        nonreturnable

            non-collectible

                nonpaying

                    nonreciprocal

                        nondeductible

                        nontaxable

No win...no gain...no I.R.S. to pay!

Nevertheless it was a super day.

Opposition Side Bets

Opposite teams plan their attack.

One at home plate whacks the bat.

Obsession to conquer second base

Observation, no time to waste

Odds favor him with a slide.

Officials say safe when they decide.

Often bets are made off on the side.

Organizations outside wager too.

Outcome paid when game is through.

Outfielders toss lands too short.

Oath to the boss not to abort.

Overwhelmed,

overtaxed,

overwrought,

overextended,

overcome,

obliterated

Odds makers now at odds and ends!

Poker Players

Piggybank emptied big time.

Plus banks withdrawn cash with a high sign

Piece of this poker action cost big bucks.

Poker tournaments are high stakes games.

Pandora's box has many participants' names.

Pedigreed to pensioners play.

Pendulum of luck sways both ways today.

Prime show time coverage of the competition.

Promotion projects nonfiction of addiction.

Propaganda prophecy tells of personal friction.

Pipe dreamer lost most hands each play.

Payout jackpot was won by another today.

Provoked player not a soothsayer, no way.

Proof was nasty fellow lost all his cash.

Pissed off left with a burr up his ass.

Quarter Slots

Quota of coins I bet less than a dollar.

Quarters are my choice

　　　　　playing for many an hour.

Quantity is all I can afford.

　　　　　more won is my reward.

　　　　　hardly ever got bored.

Quart of beer in a stein

　　　　　sometimes white wine.

　　　　　no extra cash to dine.

Quality of my life is fine.

Qualify not to cross a line.

Quantum leap to bet dollars

Quick loss of my game hours

Quandary - just play a quarter!

Quietly I give myself this order.

Rat Race

Racing through your day of life.

Recall if you lived it in strife.

Rat race's a gamble when you toss the dice.

Rainbows or thunderstorms,

Rip-roaring changes are the norms.

Rock bottom to new bright burning heights

Riding the waves of luck during the nights.

Rescued by morn's light during your flight.

Resilient roulette game your enemy

Rotated successive winning bets for me.

Rite of passage reversed bad luck to recede.

Rebounded with mucho diñero for my need.

Reason now to quit the rat-race war.

Repaid my bookie to settle the score.

Retired my gambling addiction forever more.

    now sipping a martini on a sandy shore.

Roulette

Roulette wheel *spinning,*

spiraling,

turning,

whirling,

swirling.

Round and round

slowing

stopping

Red or black upon landing

Reality to those still standing

betters

winners

gainers

losers

Received the news of their losses

Reducing or retiring

Rustle up more cash for riding.

Rose-colored glasses are worn.

Rookie optimistic as a newborn

Rewards are there for the taking

163

Resilient outlook awaiting.

Recovery of chips is a first mission.

Remember to relax and listen.

Remainder of my last remission.

Raring to bet all I have left.

Slots

Wheels spinning...

my head turning,

swirling...

whirling.

Symbols spin around and around.

Again and again...

round and round...

like perpetual motion.

So goes my emotions,

like on a wavy ocean.

Lights a-flashing, bells a-ringing

Am I a-winning?

Wishing...

praying

hoping...

That you'll be stopping on aligned bars.

landing across and all in rolls.

My money is running lower and lower.

My coins are few and nearly through.

Don't want to leave. Don't want to go.

I want to stay—yes--all day to play.

Play and play.

      'til all my money goes away.

I need to win, win, win!

            twirl your internal metal and tin.

                but have a heart!

My happiness, my joy is found within ...

          your whirling,

             circling spin.

Win for me, I plead!

Today and every day I play your slots.

Hoping to score more and lots and lots.

Handle in my sweating hand,

Janking it for winning symbols to land.

I closed my eyes to pray.

          and?

Darn! Well, tomorrow's another day to play.

Table Tactics

Tantalizing table games are for me.

Techniques I use win twofold, you'll see.

Typically I score getting much more.

Technically I play as if I'm in a winning war.

Theory of mine works every time.

Throw the dice...

        spin the wheel...

                deal the cards...

                        hit on line....

Time-tested my winning skyward soars,

                    and scores.

Top-secret I never reveal.

Track record is the real deal.

Transfixed watching the spinning wheel.

Tremendous stack of my winning chips.

Tribute to the croupiers of generous tips

Travel worldwide and change my disguise.

Truism is to avoid being denied getting inside.

Trepidation of exposure taught me to be wise.

Transcontinental trips suit me fine.

Top-notch sentimental bistros to dine

Tropical places with local fine wine.

Time to play my aces.

Tourists wheeling totes and suitcases.

Transoceanic cruises to foreign places.

Transplanting testing onboard new faces.

Transcending more jackpots without any traces.

Uncontrollable

Unaccustomed to heavy casino losses I overact

especially back to back

Undaunted I withdrew a bigger check.

Unbeknown to lose or win, so what the heck!

Ultimately believe I'll win it back and then some.

Unfortunate just bad luck, but I'm not done.

Unguarded were my plays.

Unfriendly, unlucky casino days

Uncontrollable urge to update my win

Unreasonable losses were a sin.

Utterly an action of distraction

Unacceptable useless reaction

Uproar over ... it's time to place my chips.

Unwinding, drinking martini nips and sips.

Unlimbered and ready for action

Unaware of my addiction to gamble

Unwisely toward the tables I amble.

Up-front suggestion: a question --

how about alcohol too?

Upchucking more than a sample.

Vice Versa

Vice of gambling one wishes to win mucho diñero.

Valid advice offered is the odds are narrow.

Vamoose soon reduces losses and sorrow.

Vow you made was not to borrow.

Vast losses occurring are neglecting tomorrow.

Vacation was your family's plan,

        and a suntan

          relaxing on a shore of sand.

Ventures and fun at sea and in the sun

Vice versa is if you lost and won none.

Void is your bankroll, bets lost in an undertow.

        you just couldn't say no.

Victim of gambling addictions favors no one.

Venerable ventures will vacuum up your soul.

     variance for no one.

Winners and Losers

Winning is my greatest desire!

Whirling wheels spinning I never tire.

When a ball is circling,

'round and 'round it goes.

Where it stops nobody knows.

Wishing with my eyes closed.

Waiting 'til my number showed.

Wager lost once more tonight.

Weekends, I gamble past the light of dawn.

Worn-out,

Wiped-out,

Money almost gone.

Wakeful enough to play Blackjack

Willpower is naught.

Wallet open...wild gains sought.

chips bought.

time to get my payback.

Warpath -- I'm on to triple my stack.

Warrior with cards and poker games

Working my witchcraft.

Witness my wizardly act.

Winning big are my today's aims!

Worthless cards the dealer dealt.

Wordless and wounded is how I felt.

Whipped by a welterweight or whatever.
What's more I welshed on a loan.
Wacked below my belt.

wham...

slam...

moan ...

groan...

When the dealer had a royal flush.
With my worthless aces high...lost.
Wept... and wow--did I ever cuss!
Whammy in Miami!
Went through all my cash.
Wanted to walk away loaded.
Wasted instead, fell down on my ass.
Worrying about my lack of wealth.
Welfare not enough to cover my bets
Working to me doesn't appeal.
Weakness for gambling... just can't stop.
Whatever will I do???
What's a way out with a new opt?
Wisdom is shared from those akin.
Worldwide "*Gamblers Anonymous*" is for you!
With the program free too.
Win-win is their game of life anew!

X - On The Line

X is the line you sign.

Verifying the loan for your loss.

Casino's boss warns of the interest cost.

Including the "dine and wine."

Also the payback time

Listed all the borrowers names.

Sign on the red dotted line.

Gambling -- ain't it fun and games?

Yo . . . You!

Yo!!! You want to be a winner at Blackjack?

Yours truly will show you what you lack.

Yin and yang are internalized in my lucky stars.

Yellow coins of gold and high number dollars

Yesterday bought two new luxury cars.

Yea! Won a bundle in just a few hours.

Y'all want me to teach you how?

Your cost will be discounted now.

You can't loose with me at your side

Yep! I'll be your guide.

Yawn ...you bore us both!

Yesterday we lost.

Yes, we made an oath.

Yea, not to stay

Yokels we're not!

Yield to con men, no way!

Yahooer -- just go away.

Zero

Zip, zip... dealer deals them from the deck.

got a pain in the neck.

wrote my last check.

Zero - kings and queens not in my hand.

better to be with a beer can.

Zilch, no aces too.

Zone's a war zone by the dealer's tone.

Zippy hippies lost too.

I'm through!

going home!

moan,

moan,

groan,

groan.

Zeal lost.

Zero diñero a big time cost!

Zippy-Do-Da

Zippy – do -- da... zippy – de -- yay

       casino games I play

Zany gambler expecting to win

            chances are thin.

Zestfully threw the dice

Zigzagged on the felt twice.

Zillion won?

   Never

      ever!

        None!

Zero...zip... zilch today.

   Be back the next day.

Zodiac

Zodiacal sign of mine reveals I'll win today.

Zoom-zoom, I'm speeding out to play.

Zeal is overwhelming, compelling; I can't lose.

Zigzagging to the slots, plopping on a stool.

Zillions, millions won't be won!

> Thousands will be so cool.

> Lusting just for one.

> Praying, begging

>> I begin spinning,

>> dreaming of winning,

>> pleading to my lucky stars

Zing-a-ling sounds my coins.

Zip goes the multi-table bars

> all around

> up and down

>> thundering sound

> my headache pounds

Zombielike I stare – no win this time.

> Wondering about my lucky star sign??

Zero, zip, zilch, nada won.

Zest to play, another day.

Zephyr winds, sun zenith in the sky.

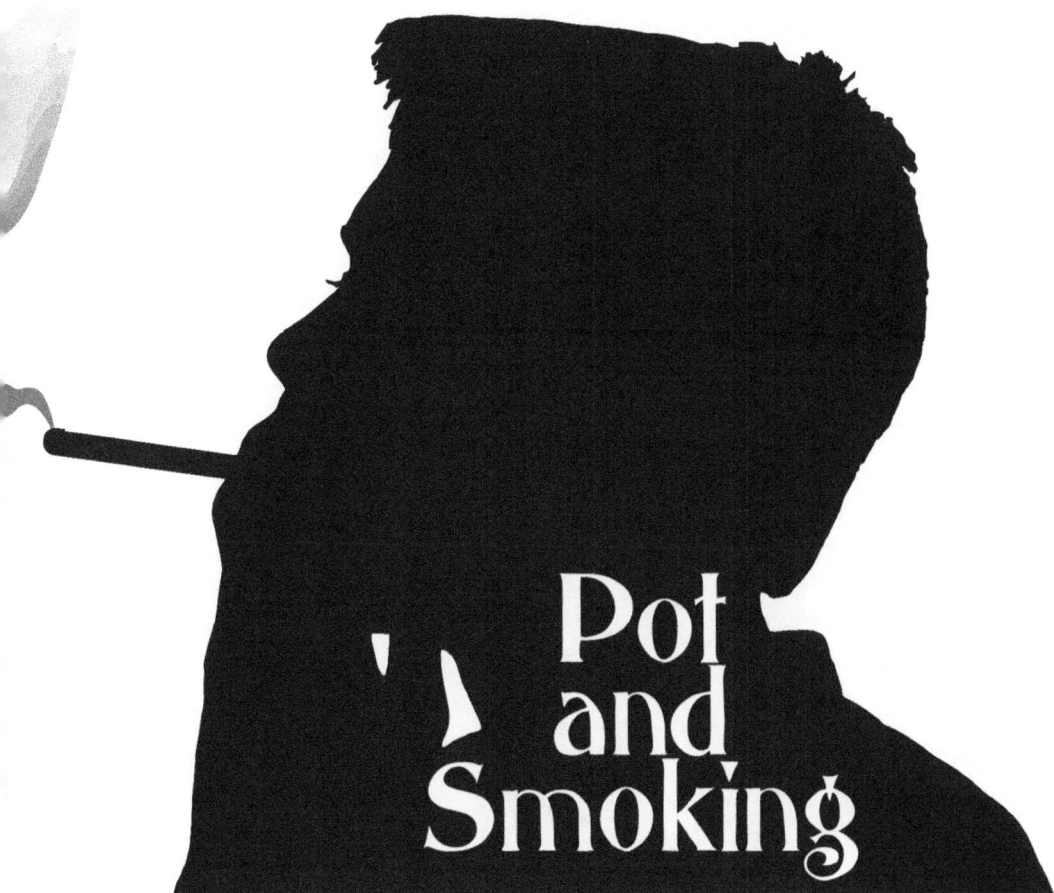

Chapter 4

Pot and Smoking

Ashes to Ashes

Ashes once rested in bottoms of ashtrays.

Ashes of cremation are buried in yesterdays.

Asinine abuse caused from smoking or toking.

Ambulance too late.

        death doesn't wait!

Aspirations of smokers challenged by expiration.

Agenda canceled to an underground forever vacation.

Addiction to tobacco was a death invitation.

Alternative was to cease smoking.

Autopsy verified toxic nicotine body invasion.

Ashes to ashes...

Butts

Blew your last puff

Bronchitis makes you huff

But you light up another ciggy.

Back to back smoker

Bingeing like a piggy.

Butts in every ashtray.

Breath smells the same.

Byline in obituaries soon one day.

Bypassed living years

Breezes whish away family's tears.

Bottom of a grave he does stay.

Chain Smoking

Cigarettes, cigars and chew contain tobacco.

Chronic smoker's choice is to die young.

Cancer of the lungs, tongue or throat.

Coronary also gets a big vote.

Count that triple if you toke

or use coke.

Choice was made with every puff.

Craving tobacco continuously.

Clinical compulsion never enough.

Chain smoking done consciously.

Cowards don't try quitting!

Determination

Detoxification of nicotine a destruction devil

Discovering you're involved in several:

> D.U.I.'s
>
> dipsomaniac
>
> devices
>
> diagnosis
>
> depression
>
> discontent
>
> distraught
>
> despair
>
> disgusted
>
> dysfunction
>
> dying
>
> divorce
>
> dependency

Decide which curse to work on first to defeat.

Double whammy of a drunkard and smoker, often both

Downhill direction needs protection to beat.

Difficult when a distraught one dismisses an oath.

Dependency of addiction diagnosis can be defeated.

Disciplined action is definitely needed.

Devices as nicotine patches or medications

Depression with patient's meds offer restorations.

Dedications made to rid defecations, to cleaner air.

Discontent with being in dysfunction or despair?

Develop and practice healthy new habits.

Demolish demonic ways all days with patience.

D.U.I.'s and divorces are by a court invitation.

Defense deliberation with deposition won.

Destruction overrun.

Destiny a new...*reformation*

                    restoration

                        revelation

                            revivification.

Determination led to recovery of another one!

Equinox

Equinox creates a time passage of day and night.

Equator crossed by the sun is an equalizer.

Episode equalizes both day and night.

Embrace this lesson of Mother Nature.

Earthlings have numerous choices.

Engagement in smoking damages voices.

Enlightenment is essential to make one wiser.

Eventuality evaluate your own morality.

Epitaph offers no resurrection.

External and internal self-destruction.

Execution of oneself is not a vision.

Explanation not needed...it's your decision!

Fixation

Frequency of smoking increases

Forenoon, afternoon and night

Forward into morn's first light

Frenzy oncoming never ceases.

Fixation addiction ignores

Full of forlorn noises--

    gag

        hack

           choke

              wheeze

                cough.

Future has recovery choices.

Fraternity together has voices.

Friendly free groups for quitting

Find one! No more rhinoshitting!

Grass, Weed, Cannabis

Got grass, got rollers, get high!

Giddy after the ounce I did buy.

Ghetto was where I was raised.

Gangs I belonged to those days.

Genius in school despite getting high.

Graduation day I smoked a joint or two.

Grades put me on the top of the class.

GED. got me a fat college scholarship.

Gave up my grass now I'm through.

Great grades through my god-given gift.

Gutter life

        fighting with a knife

        emotions in strife

Guzzling gin

Gave it up along with another sin.

Guts and genetics set me free.

Gave my studies all of me.

Goal I invested in is a lifetime win.

Habitual Smokers

History of continuous smoking plagues you?

Hocus pocus words nagging you aren't new.

Hunch you tried mostly everything to stop.

However nothing worked to date.

   never is it too late!

Human beings have brains to think.

Hurdles in life are always there.

Hurting yourself by smoking isn't an opt.

Harness your odorous stink.

Haven for all others and you is clean air.

Health cannot be bought by wealth.

Head stone's waiting if you fail.

Hipposhit fell on you like hail.

   so does family's wail.

Indiscreet Smoking

Indiscreet whiffs of foul smoke circle the air.

Where?

Everywhere!

Incurring nicotine odors fill the room.

Inconsiderate smokers care less we assume.

Irritating our lungs with their gloom and doom.

Issues nonsmokers have are blatantly ignored.

Indignation... we protested and expressed!

Incumbent officials passed a law across the board.

Incontestable that smokers now have to go outside.

Interference with our medical health is out the door.

Interdiction at last they do abide.

Interior smoking is no more.

Jinxed

Jinxed, you got cancer of the throat.

Justified because you smoke or toke.

Jolted when you received the bad news.

Juvenile when you started it and booze.

Jump-started that jumbo hipposhit when young.

Jaw,

  jowl

    throat

Judging medical records black is your lung

Joints and juice spread cancer to the tongue.

Junior, your life is over and done!!

Kin and Kids

Kids puffing and huffing on ciggies or weed.

Kinfolks need to be aware, declare and lead.

Keeping track of what their kids are doing.

Know what these young "angels" are pursuing.

Kick them in the ass when needed?

Kisses and hugs to them when not using.

Kudos and praises when not abusing.

Keep in mind cancer is not amusing!

Know How to Quit Tobacco?

Know-it-all... are you sure?

Kept your vow of cessation?

Kaput went your tobacco cure!

Kind of lost your dedication to stop!

Kinfolks say you lost your patience.

Keep on trying is always an opt.

Kick-start a new campaign with fervent desire.

Kindle it with all your passion and flaming fire.

Kiss smoking forever goodbye without a sigh.

This time...don't lie!

Legalize Charlotte's Web

Legalize medical marijuana, a deliberating debate.

Lofty arguments burden every state.

Long-winded government officials make the ill wait.

Licensing issues is one of their games.

Leading the sick down dead end lanes.

Labyrinth...*winding*

> twisting
>
> wandering
>
> curving
>
> meandering
>
> detaining
>
> restraining
>
> lingering

Leading to a nowhere path created by opponents.

Lethargic legislation lazing munches on doughnuts?

Let empowered cannabis supporters be proactive.

Launch massive messages of e-mail

and snail mail.

Later than sooner is the officials' repeated tale.

Lawmakers are sitting dozing on their tails.

Leeway of decision-making overdue.

Legitimization of weeds to pass through.

Leniency addresses those in daily severe pains.

Locomotion needed now, no more stalling games.

Late of time, politely asking for solutions is our aim.

Legislations awaiting decisions....when?

Loosey-goosey delays have to end.

[author is netural on subject]

Marijuana

Motivation for weed is for different reasons.

Medically it can improve ones ills.

Morphine not needed or dozens of pills.

Medicinal it's beneficial to many who use.

Myriads of smokers rarely abuse.

Marijuana's used for millennia of seasons.

Moderation use seems to be the norm.

Motivation becomes an impulse for a hit.

Minutes later a roll-up is leisurely lit.

Multiple-choice for those in a dorm.

Maintenance has self levels of intoxication.

Misconduct mistake of pot use and no graduation.

Nicotine and Teens

Newscast revealed many hazards of nicotine.

Numerous children smoked before thirteen.

No one cares to listen to statistics.

or unseen mystics.

Nieces and nephews, daughters and sons

Naturally ignore advice from parental ones.

Neath the need to smoke is a kid unsteady.

Naked truth, it's an addiction already.

Neglectful attitude of a healthy lifestyle

Nutritional eating is mostly overlooked.

Numskull kid on cigarettes or weed is hooked.

Nervous system all the while...

awry

hyper

anxious

jittery

tense

Note: hair, clothes, mouth smell foul as bile.

Neurotic behavior is no surprise.

Nincompoop naïve kids tell lies.

Nagging at them isn't wise.

Naturally kids by spite will do otherwise.

Negotiations with them may help.

Never ever whip with a leather belt.

Nor bribe them with your wealth.

Note: quitting will be by their selves.

Obstacles of Smoking

Obstacles for smoking or toking-

Only are yours alone!

Opinion is just my own.

Ordering you not to,

    no one is your boss here.

Only you alone!

Organizations can tell you what to fear.

Obsession need courage to conquer it.

Overwhelmed by life, ciggies not an answer.

Oppressed

Or depressed doesn't stop igniting cancer.

Objective is to rid your excuses of rhinoshit!

Option is yours alone.

Ordeal of nicotine ingestion creates ills.

Oral cancers too with many bills.

Or a favorite target is the lung.

Odious odor oozing from the tongue.

Opaque vile smells coat your mouth.

Ordure envelopes clothes and body.

Others around say you're stinky like a potty.

Offer your loved one an ashtray kiss.

Outhouse lips that are gross.

Other words, something desired to miss!

Outlook for smokers are dim or slim.

Opposite direction medically you may win.

Opponent to stopping tobacco

        – or you're burnt toast.

Obliterate slimy lies and whys you won't stop.

Opt to quit per medical advice.

Otherwise a cemetery is a dead end trip!

Only you are tossing the dice!

Outcome awaiting may be your crypt.

Pot and Prudes

Passionate need for pot all day long?

People can say smoking pot is wrong.

Probability straight-laces who never tried.

Proponents against pot tend to abide.

Probably damning the opposite side.

Puking up gobs of their poison phlegm.

Persnickety anti-petitions solicited by them.

Philanthropy is to help not condemn.

Pot smokers may be ill or disabled.

Persons using pot should not be labeled.

Point is:

        reason of using may be their health.

Please,

        keep unsolicited opinions to yourself.

Prohibition isn't for the big mouths to say.

Prognosis is done in a medical way.

Professionals have free programs

Providing help for

    cessation

        dependence

stopping

quitting

Pursuant to also undertake other stands

those without bans.

Participants may get nicotine replacements.

Proof warranted for these other devices

patches,

lozenges,

nicotine gum,

medical pot.

Programs' purposes are for supportive advices

also legal prescriptions

if required for addiction.

Promoting caring and helping and healings.

Prudish provokers have you no feelings?

Quash Secondhand Smoking

Quickly upwind billows streaming smoke.

Wisps rising with each exhale

silently twisting,

whirling,

swirling,

caught by the wind.

Quietly captured into the air

polluting,

poisoning,

putrefying,

lungs of those close by.

Secondhand smoke of throats so bare

gasping for air.

Smokers don't seem to care.

Streaming vile nicotine everywhere.

Qualms nonexistent for habitual users of tobacco

huffing,

puffing,

snorting,

smokers just don't care.

blowing... contaminating... air everywhere.

contaminating everyone's air.

201

Quitting Smoking

Quitting smoking is hard to do.

Quandary of what and how to pursue

Question? When to stop?

Quit before your lungs are:

        begging

          gasping

            coughing

              wheezing

Qualifications needed –reread the above.

Query also includes –potential cancer

      of the throat

        of the lungs

          of the mouth

Quid chewing is included too.

Quid pro quo - give up smoking or your life.

Rehabilitation

Rehabilitated to your former health.

Rumor is you quit smoking by yourself.

Rough going at first, I heard.

Rejected bravely not to continue the absurd.

Remember how many times you quit?

Realized how important live is worth.

Read through all the medical reports

Reformed from inhaling puffs or snorts.

Reaction was to value living your life.

Relationship improved with family and wife.

Rejuvenated by your love more often.

Result is <u>you're not</u> in a satin coffin.

Resting eternally encased in mother earth.

Resurrected is liken to rebirth.

Smoking

$\mathcal{S}$moke shelters you from life's stresses?
Stupid thinking of shortsighted guesses.
Shovelful of rhinoshit thrown in your face.
Smacked the smelly stuff there for you to taste.
Swallow it all with haste without any waste.
Smokey mouth to others smelly like shit.
Shamelessly blowing putrid smoke everywhere.
Smothering your body with poisoned air.
Small-minded smokers do you care?
Smelly smoke

       smothering,

       smogging,

       settling,

       scumming

         everywhere.
Skedaddled away from reality of your case.
Satisfied your addictive taste,

         by all the money you waste.
Sabotage your own life, but not others, please!
Saccharine smile stated tobacco relieves stress.
Sorry, facts prove nicotine addicts die young.
Soon you'll be underground at rest too.
Sadly sanity had deserted you.

       so true to one with poo-poo on the tongue.

204

Tackling Tobacco

Tackling tobacco use is to sideline withdrawal signs.

Touchdown is scoring across the goal lines.

Taking defensive measures

To stop that pass

        is the linebacker's task.

Target is the chain smoking receiver.

Tobacco is a vice of his obsessions

Toking marijuana is first, not last.

Tequila is another of his passions.

Testosterone compensates for neither.

Talent is subdued by his tranquilizer use,

        another addictive abuse.

Tavern shots were nonstop last night.

Toking, smoking, drinking 'til he was tight.

Tipsy, tumbling into a taxi high as a kite.

Threw up 'til morning's first light.

Trust me; he's unfit for todays game!

Tickets sold, fans seated.

Team's taken their positions.

Transition from play conditions.

Transposing as needed.

Tandem play in action

Trembling sensations in his hands.

Throw of his was wildly un-aimed.

                    ball twisted

              twirled

Toss landed in the grand stands.

Thrice more he fumbled,

                    stumbled,

                staggered.

Tipsy player was bad enough

Toking marijuana joints and other stuff

Taken out of the game,

Threw up on his way to being benched.

Treatment center he must enter!

Termination or rehab for this lad.

Tenacious teammates scored and scored.

Tidings... without the bum, they won by one.

Undertaker

Uncanny undertaking at the morgue this morn.

Unconscious smoker being prepped for viewing

Unexpectedly dying young was of corpse's own doing.

Unluckily, daily inhaled second smoke when born.

Umpteen years went by, unwisely began the habit too.

Unreasonable packs ripped open and torn.

Unsealed one new pack after the other.

Upbringing learned from dad and mother.

Useless to quit for mood becomes too forlorn.

Unsafe to smoke the doctors did warn.

Unheeded the medical advice.

Undertaker has the body on ice.

Underground now in an urn.

Understand... addiction is something you learn.

Unenlightened? Go ahead and *take your turn.*

Unearth a curse learned on planet earth.

Universally, the nonsmoking alien race is wise.

Unhealthy earthlings to them are not a surprise!

Vamping E-Cigarettes

Vampires insert their fangs for a nightcap of blood sucking.

Vampers' choice is smokeless nicotine vapor inhaling.

Vodka and vino drinkers tend to get tipsy and wasted.

Various addictions and habits are, or by choice, medical needs.

Viewpoint on "charlotte's web," usage remains debatable.

Valuation waits medical values on these altered weeds

Venomous cigarettes, well known for its 7000 poisons.

Vapors of toxins sucked deep into your lungs,

        vile odor coating your tongue.

Vice you choose will be voluntary.

Vamping is a new rage

        quit, in this addictive age.

        Wean off the nicotine,

        very cautioned for teens!

        E-cigs come in tasty flavors –

        chocolate to grape –

        candy tastes to go ape.

Vaporized nicotine inhaled by battery power.

Vamp e-cigs may help one quit.

Victorious and a ciggy victim no more

Visualize yourself free from that vile shit!

Vital statistics now's a higher score!

Verdict is no voodoo, just stay unlit!

Vampires and Smoking

Vampires suck your juicy blood.

Venomous tobacco products vexes

Viceful habit sucks away your life.

Virgin veins vulnerable to nicotine crud.

Vampires and ciggies both have a nexus.

Venomous poisons invaded vessels.

Validated diseases in both sexes.

Vying to take your life away.

Vaporized smoke in lungs made you pay.

Vault in a cemetery is where you lay.

Vapor Trails

Validated reasons for why you smoke, you claim.

Virile macho manly is one reason.

Vulnerable to wheezing is that part of your game?

Vowels slurred when coughing up your name.

Voice rattles with variability...cough

cough

cough.

Varies with your hacking...

violently,

vehemently

vibrantly

Vapor trail absorbed and attacking,

throat

mouth

lungs

Villain is yourself.

Vendetta is between you and your smokes.

Vote for health not for your totes.

View it as a vice- I say it twice vice-vice!

Voice it only as my advice.

That's all folks!

Why Smoke?

Why are you still smoking?

    toking?

        coking?

            weeding?

When you declared to quit last night,

    never again *a ciggy* to light.

Warp-speed you lit up, no hesitation,

    no waiting,

    no delaying,

    no postponing.

Walked out of the doctors office vowed to quit ...

                hipposhit!

Work-up clarified and verified.

Why aren't you terrified?

Warned of dangers of your nicotine habit.

Welfare now at a critical state,

Wellbeing can not wait.

Waste not a second more.

Withdrawal means winning the tobacco war!

Whoever's wheezing to their core.

Willpower will guide you through.

Willy-nilly is not a way out!

　　it's for those who are;

　　　　weaklings,

　　　　wishy-washy,

　　　　wavering,

　　　　wailing,

　　　　weaseling,

　　　　whining.

Whatever excuses just won't work!

Well-advised by medical statistics to quit.

　　your excuses can't be given;

　　if you want to keep on living!

Where and when to start is today with action.

Waste can is on your way out,

　　toss all tobacco, weed, and whatever,

　　to the bottom forever.

Welcome to living and winning!

White elephant no longer sitting on your heart,

　　　nor squeezing your lungs of air, not now.

Without smoking now you're smart!!!

Withdrawal

Weakness of smoking used to be mine.

Weary of coughing or being winded.

Withdrawal then resumed in no time.

Wafting odor spiraling in the wind...

Waft of smoke set me on again.

Wonder if I can reach an end.

Waiting to quit for good.

Why wait? I know I could!

Warned I should!

Want my healthy life back.

Weapon is my willpower.

Week after week I will attack.

      Hour after hour,

        minute by minute,

Whatever it takes to win it.

      Wheezing fading,

        coughing subsiding,

Whim of not dying.

Wish worked with self control.

Wonder if it was my alphabet soup bowl?

X- Rays of Your Lungs

X-rays of your lungs tell it all.

       Should have, could have, too late.

       Doctor warned to quit, don't stall.

       Nothing can be done or won anymore.

       Medical tests shows cancer to your core.

       Disease war, a battle lost.

       Smoking was the cost.

X-rays verified it's way too late.

       Quitting leaves no time to wait!

Yours Truly

Yesterdays of before, yours truly was a smoker.

Yea, but more so was a cougher and choker.

Yarn I tell is never liked smoking very well.

Youthful teen was I when joining the crowd.

Yattered about things that didn't matter

Yesteryear fitting in was said out loud.

Ying and yang was not yet in style.

Yielding to temptation without denial

           part of my tale...

           I didn't even inhale...

           taste was foul and stale.

Yearned to stop smoking and choking.

           no, I'm not at all joking.

Yearbook showed I was popular in the group.

Yen to opt to stop; we all smelled like poop.

Yes I quit...that's no *rhinoshit.*

Yo...you there ...see I'm unlit.

Yuck, yuck, yuck!

           Smoking sucks!

Zero Tolerance

Zero tolerance is simply that!

"No smoking" says the posted sign.

Zilch tobacco use!

Café where we wine and dine,

no one can light up there!

Therefore, no odoriferous air.

Kind smokers go to puff outside.

We're thankful they abide!

Chapter 5

Hodgepodge

Addiction of Running

*W*as it first the sun I felt?

warm, radiant

upon my barren shoulders.

or... was it the wind?

caressing against my panting

cheeks and fervent brow?

Bending the pine and palm leaves

in reverence with a bow.

I remember it not.

Wondering if it was the scent of eucalyptus

yesterday or now?

Was it when running with soft sinking sand

under barren feet

(having shed my Nike elites)

yielding to miles

of imprints upon the shore?

or... was it seeing, in flight the seagull

through *azul* skies soar?

I remember it not.

When was it?

running against the ocean's horizon

capturing each last second

before today turned to night

'till the glowing sun was out of sight

'till streaked fingers of rose and tinged yellow

blended into the midnight of night?

I was then...

    motionless

    standing

    shuttering

in the streaming moonlight

Anxious for tomorrow's newborn dawn.

Knew running penetrated my every pore,

Became my love forever more!

Bargains

Bargains are what I look for.

Because, why pay more?

Bagfuls of my buys in my shopping cart

Bought tons of clothes before.

Buying now accessories to match.

Basket is filling with handbags and shoes.

Boutique booth has oodles to choose.

Browsing now through the purse aisles

Boggles my mind at all the styles.

Beige leather tote is to die for

     into the cart.

Basic black shoulder bag

Bows on the toes, sandals score

Black and beige stilettoes can't be ignored

    hoard, hoarding, hoarded...

    added to the cart.

Ballerina-beaded flats a work of art

    placed into the cart.

Bound next, to jewelry counter

        then I go bonkers more or less.

Breathtaking is a blue sapphire necklace...

Bewitching me from its velvet case.

Budget is likely blown!

But this is one gem I have to own.

Besides it matches my cultivated taste.

Blinded by a sparkling emerald ring

Behind the pearl earrings in the display case.

But best not to buy another thing.

Better to leave and go home.

Bank balance states I am broke!

Behavior of splurging was my mine alone.

Bargains aren't bargains if you'll need a loan.

Closets Overstuffed

Closets overstuffed and my drawers too.

Clothes are my addiction.

Constantly need to buy something new.

Catharsis for me, my shrink said, is my shopping.

Commercial shops or yard sales, I'm always stopping.

Cut-rate sales I can't ignore.

Customer credit cards at every store

Cash also will do.

Cramming my buys into every closet space.

Clearances bought fit into a tight place.

Closeouts are a must. I can't get enough!

Clutter control is needed for my stuff,

so I:

condensed,

squeezed,

stuffed,

stashed,

sectionized,

segmentized,

selectized,

all that I buy.

Color coordination is a must.

Clothes are sorted from small to large.

Why?

Certainly want to keep my pre-diet wardrobe still.

Contingency is, heaven forbid, if I gain weight again.

Contemptible fatty pounds, I refuse with all my will.

Counting calories I put to an end.

Curvaceous and now an attractive size ten.

Corpulence I have no more.

Coped with blubber once before

Clothes, large in size,

> kept as a reminder,
> of my being wise,
> to win my fatso war.

Clothes horse, I won't deny.

Continue to buy, buy, and buy!

Consider me to be a shopaholic to my core!

> Yes, I admit to be,
> and add "hoarder"
> to my disorder.

Chances I'll find sales still at the malls' stores.

Cognitively, there's no more storage space

Cause I'll find some place.

Credit card in hand, off I go,

so don't get on my case!

Dogs, Cats and Other Critters

Divorce my dog?

Deprive me from devoted bow wow?

Delirium or dementia hit you somehow?

Or are you sipping spiked eggnog?

Decision would be a doomsday scenario.

Disaster of mega proportions

'Druther divorce my mate

Decision that really I'd hate

Decry that I'd have to decide

Dogs of many breeds

    poodles

        spaniels

            pitbulls

                terriers

                    shepherds

Dote on all of my dozen and one.

Dread to get rid of even one!

Dachshund will never go to a pound.

Dalmatians are spotted all around.

Cats

Dictate for me to get rid of my cats.

Dilemma I can't envision.

Depression I'll suffer from that decision.

Devoted we're to each other

Determined to keep all ten of them.

Despicable conversation is at the end!

Critters

Did you call me an animal lover?

Definite conclusion is I care for my pets

Daily custodian not of my significant other, but

Dalmatians, rabbits, falcon, a dove or two

Demand all my attention.

Dedicated to all of them my full affection.

Dolphins would have been too...

Don't have a seacoast inlet to my pool.

Doubtful if I can deal with anything more.

Domesticated are only some you see.

Drawing the line to what I can handle.

Dozen of slithering snakes are not for me.

Donkey or two . . . destiny? Maybe . . . might be?

Note: Daughter Lolin used to rescue dogs and horses.

227

Electronics

Eliminate entertainment, what then?

End electronic games?

what's next?

Effects will complex and hex

teens won't function

nor have any gumption

nor any aims.

End electricity then what, when?

Entire planet in an entire blackout

East to west and everywhere is panic.

Earthlings begin to behave manic.

Emergency status is transatlantic.

Everyone asks who here can tell

– is this the ending?

– who can say?

– heading for hell?

Downward?

Descending?

Exponents of science explain we'll all be well.

Evidence of explosion of worldwide computers

Evildoers loose are those who are looters.

Episode in entirety was from a teenage game.

Enterprising bold move blew out every fuse.

Engineered web product was the blame.

Extraordinary kid created "the game" online.

Excited nations gave him a contract to sign.

Extraterrestrials' Visit

Extraterrestrials' view of us earthlings.

Elements needed here are carbon and water.

Emotions are energy wasteful distasteful disorders.

Environment borders on uninvited invading warfare.

Everywhere is chaos and disease with babies crying.

Everywhere the planet is covered with polluted air.

Everyday humans from east to west are dying.

Estimate of their overpopulation is understated.

Earthlings are unreliable and unregulated.

Economy, infrastructure, ecosystem beyond repair

Education is lacking with students who don't care.

Ethnic groups have hesitation to mingle

Erroneous nation even when single.

Eating habits often to gross excess.

Exercises too much or too less

Elects for suicide with addictive alcohol use

Eden never had drugs, tobacco or booze.

E-mailing eliminates personal conversations.

Experiments to win or lose their cash.

Expected a royal flush at casinos a serious task.

Enema flush needed up player's ass.

Earthlings' planet may not last!

Followers and Leaders

Foreign to you to be a leader

    or a front-wheeler.

Frontiersmen are bold and brave

    others are only a slave.

Futuristic leaders show the right way.

Freedom-fighters keep enemies at bay.

Freemasons were here before and today.

Funeral directors direct deceased to lay.

Futurologists lead humans to a righteous new way.

Furthermore as a follower you have little to say.

God Given Genetics?

Yesterday's miles, added on to my goal,

rain or shine I train.

I fear not bad weather's toll.

Need to train for my marathon race.

More miles to build up my base

Weight I tend not to gain, and stay the same

Calories I burn like fire.

Because I run, run, run 'til I tire.

Slim and trim--a hot muscle machine.

Swift as a tiger--lean and mean.

heed my mighty roar,

bellowing from my inner core.

At the finish line, yes I'll be sore.

Distances I run might seem insane.

My genetics do carry the blame.

Workout every day

How many hours I can't say,

Running to, running from.

I'm just a racing bum.

Waiting for daylight to come

Lacing up my training shoes,

                then I dash out the door.

Run, run, 'til I'm sore.

Admitting can't do no more.

At dawn I'll start again.

Sprinting toward the shore

Spending daylight 'til the sun bends

Into the waves beyond yonder sea

Dipping rosy fingers 'til you can't see.

God lends me each day to spend.

Thanks...to my higher power I send,

For my life god loans me 'til my end.

Hoarding

Hoarded for countless years.

Have stacks, piles in high towers.

Heartbreaking mementos bringing tears

However, with it comes past sorrows.

Harum-scarum memories of a time before

Haunt me deeply to my inner core.

Hack and bore away to a furrowed grove.

Hitting, levitating the scared wound.

Hiding from my past is why, if you must ask.

House perched on a hilly cove was my move.

Hunkered inside stashing my things far and wide.

Hyper all the time hurling things flying past

Huddled in my favorite corner at last.

Humongous gathered junk piled high

seems like as high as the sky.

Hindsight hints my hoarding is an homage

Hindered myself to retake my own house,

with no complaints from every mouse.

Hypothesis leads to teenage years,

shedding hysterical tears.

Hypnosis may unravel why I hoard so much.

Have hissy fits and such.

Internet Identity

Incognito is what I prefer to be.

Invisible, no one staring at me.

Internet is how I flirt and date.

Inhibitions are lost online.

        because I can hide

            my immense weight.

Infatuation of my heart...

Identification if live, I can't disguise

            my huge size.

Intermittent diets, lost then regained.

Intimidated by my big oversize.

              sight unseen is safe I figure.

Intriguing and alluring I can appear

If invisible and no one's near.

Insulated by online dating,

Innocuous intimate feeling I can express.

In isolation I am introspective and do confess.

Insured by my computer screen

              sight unseen

           one only can guess

              more or less.

Internet can lie if I'm obese or thin and lean.

Junk Collector

Jigsaw puzzle is wherever you hide junk.

Just smell from whence wafts the stunk.

Jab here and there finding trash everywhere.

Judgment is failing your mind – bad bad sign!

Jumbo jumble of hoarding of every kind.

Jock strap, joystick, juggle balls

        heaped against the walls

Jungle gym, junk mail, jeep wheels

Jam-packed against your bargain deals.

Jail-like is the room

        full of dark gloom.

Jettison that junk hazard soon!

Kleptomaniac

Knowledge of how to flat out steal.

Knock-offs are not on my shopping list.

Keepsakes are from stores where I stole.

Khaki knapsack on my back.

Kleptomania is what some call me.

Krept into places without a key.

Kind of like, friends don't suspect

Kinfolks respect that I'm high tech

Knack of know-how I do have.

Kidnap the merchandise with a grab.

Keep on avoiding the nab or the "$" tab.

Kleptomaniac is my "dare devil disease".

Kindled and a stealer of things as I please.

Liposuction and Methods

Lose those excess pounds with a quick fix?

Liposuction's real or a trick?

Laser body contouring?

Laboratory body occurring?

Lopsided or curving?

Love affair with yourself?

Low self-esteem?

Lotions and potions didn't work?

Lumpty, humpty, dumpty you felt.

     Too tight is your belt.

Lifeline needed with medical help!

Lunacy felt and you went berserk.

Lump sum you paid to doctor jerk.

Lose your obesity if you choose.

*Logic one...*is also to lose the booze.

*Logic two...*is be health wise.

Look at your bulging size.

Loose clothing just doesn't disguise.

Let's get wise!

Logic three ...

Lethal major health problems exist

Likelihood you're on this list:

      heart disease

      stroke

      diabetes

      high blood pressure

      elevated cholesterol

      depression

      skin disease

      sleep disorder

      headaches

      life's longevity

Look and pick out what you want.

Landfill of food you ate returns to haunt.

Last rites you'd certainly hate.

Life insurance a liability with excess weight!

Lose that blubber before it's too late.

Layers of fat tissue from what you ate.

      tick tock is the time bomb clock.

      Don't ask me more- ask the Doc!

Listen to the doc., *tick tock* goes your clock!!!

Marathon Runner

Barefoot impressions on the shores' sand,

conquering a mile more of earths ' land.

Spanning the gap of time and space,

Banning hours not to waste,

'till the seagulls faded from sight

replaced by a velvet night.

Tides will come to cover my footsteps ran;

...over each beach dune,

of every afternoon.

Marathon race will come soon.

sand imprints of a long distance run

summers casts my muscles tan by sun.

A sunrise awaits tomorrow,

'tis another day I may borrow.

Mirror, Mirror

Mirror, mirror on yonder wall,

      Do tell me who's the fairest of all?

Truth you must tell.

   No lies.

No wise ass truth in disguise.

Does my beauty still fare well?

Tell me... tell me now!!!

Tell me as I look into your glass.

What I see is your beauty of once upon a time,

      Now faded into the past.

Your reflection shows of beauty not to last.

Within my mirror, I see line after line.

Years have not been kind

A face once radiant

      Once so fair

Time brought lines and wrinkles to wear

      For your mind to bear.

A glimmer of loveliness still reigns now.

      Pains and lines embedded your brow.

Wrinkles from a frown are everywhere.

Years in the golden sun, so tranquil,

so warm

Changed your face.

Without kindness or grace.

Which is now the case.

Satin and lace can't change age,

nor wrinkles erase,

from yesterdays or now...

from smile to brow.

Diamonds, pearls lend only their grace

but don't change your face.

Smile lines and frowns from past years,

along with joys and tears,

left impressions ...lines of time.

Signs of aging...

gently touched your cheeks,

Implanted such kisses upon rosy lips.

Results of ravages of time took place.

Wrinkles of the eyes,

Sun burned face,

Blemishes of thin skin.

242

All blended in worry and strife.

These lines are no disgrace.

They're there to bear,

Passage of your life you wear.

Occurred with years and tears.

despite loving care.

Yet behold...never lose your smile

throughout the next years.

Net-Text and E-Mail

Networking can twist us into a social disorder.

Nationwide it exists both inside and outside.

Nowadays without boundary or border.

Newfangled electronics rule us worldwide.

Navigating, negotiating, nightclubbing...

Not to forget business, education, transportation

Nucleus of our lives depends on this new relation.

Numerous inventions became our nirvana sensation.

Now the nitty-gritty truth is we can't do without.

No-brainer if you look all around everywhere.

Non-personal communication is what it's all about.

Neutral information as if they didn't care to share.

Obstacles

Obstacles
are only lessons
teaching you courage
along life's way.

Obstacles
are the strengthening tools
for self-survival
in your journey.

Own them;
don't allow them
to own you!

Online Obsessive Disorder

Often I shop by computer at home;

Occupying my time home all alone.

Opportunity is so easy to buy clothes online.

Obsessive occupation is my astrological sign.

Obviously, it's an overwhelming habit of mine.

Officially, it's an obsessive-compulsive disorder.

Opinions from others I ignore!

Oppression from them is only their depressions.

Other words, they're jealous of my possessions.

Organized is my closet...

        Whoops-closets...

        All is hung in color-coordinated order.

Overstuffed drawers neatly arranged too.

Obstacle was once of being obese before

        then I didn't fit through any door,

        halted my buying sprees.

        That's when I began my diet war.

Overheard talk of my obese size,

        Alerted me to get calorie wise.

Overweight-sized ass overwhelmed guys.

Overt laughter and outright teases

Oracles forecast the same.

Only I am to blame.

Omen from a dove warned me.

No excuse or a lie.

Diet or die!

That is why.

Vision of mine is...

Overpowering,

overwhelming,

obscure,

opaque,

ominous,

Overcast skies,

cloudy,

misty,

hazy,

maybe I'm crazy!

Outer space I'm in.

Otherworldly beings surround me.

Overindulgence of food was my only sin.

Outcome of my gorging was I didn't win!

Obituary notice sent by a dove.

247

Overeating was her greatest love.

Oodles of flesh were the cost.

Open-heart surgery failed!

She lost.

Opened my eyes from the opiate of my dreaming.

Optimum action was to diet with no more scheming.

Overawed by my new life now.

Wow!!!

Only once I was fat as a cow.

Overcame that years ago.

Awake now...and back online

Overtime I spend to buy...

at a grand -opening place.

Outright I won't lie, if asked why.

Overboard I admit to my obsession of clothes.

Others do too, with good taste.

Outlet boutique is of outer space

Outfit in blue, size six, is my newest find.

Observing what's next while sipping a glass of wine.

How sublime!!!

Only By Personal Permission

Only I alone can give my permission...

for my addiction!

Be it that of alcohol or drugs:

or stuffing my body

gobbling gobs of food,

alas...minus nutrition.

Or by gambling 'til broke.

at casinos when in a betting mood.

Overdo my smoking too.

Adding more plays resulting in subtraction

love the action with passion!

Alas, have no chips to cash in.

Lost today, but someday I'll win.

so at break time sneak in a toke.

Tobacco or weed is another habit.

usually when I use

results in over abuse.

Puff puffs the magic dragon...

when on or off the wagon.

Exhaling-cough, cough, cough.

Obsession of computers or other electronics toys

        are my lifestyle's main frame on and off.

        using 'til I'm nearly blind.

Outcome soon is it's gin or wine time.

Otherwise am in outer space.

     Pampering me and my psyche.

     Locked in cyberspace

     my time there is not of waste.

       Perpetually producing a frame of sublime.

        Permission I grant me, all the time.

Odds are that physically and mentally I'm hooked.

Obtained by my permission

Obsession by my addiction!

Pack Rat

Packages are yet unopened,

          hoarded,

               stashed everywhere.

Purchased by somebody who doesn't care.

Places to store them all are running short.

Picture a warehouse jammed with mostly junk.

Pack rat won't even arrange them or sort.

Place overrun with an obnoxious stunk.

Possibly worse than a rotting skunk.

Paradox is...who died in the trunk?

Quickie Haiku

Quintessence is a quest.

Quantum leap no test.

Question is: who is the best?

Running

Bending low to tie my shoelace

Breaking in new shoes, just my size.

Ready for my daily exercise.

Miles ahead, my intention's ne'er to waste

Hot sunny day means a slower pace,

  to be added to my base.

Tired still from yesterdays fast race.

Obsession of running is my idyllic taste.

No way, an intervention!

So don't get on my case,

  or in my face,

  got no time to waste.

Shopaholic

Shopaholic is my addiction, but what a pleasure.

Shop 'til you drop is my motto.

love it, don't you?

me too!

Spending sprees I look forward to.

Stimulating all my pores

shivering with goose bumps

I want to buy more, more, and more.

Sales - I'm first at store

Super sales - I'm first thru the door

Split second later I found the dress of the century

Slid to a screeching halt at shoes near the entry

Shopping is so much fun, honey.

Spending all my money.

Scintillating pure pleasure.

Salvation from too much leisure

Scanned the next aisle

Scored a seductive silk scarf next,

Screaming of sensuous sex.

Soiree next week, I need a new evening dress.

Splurged for the very best.

Some day…I may quit.

Sit at home and knit?

Shopping's my cure

   against my boozing lure.

  But if or when I no longer shop

Scotch awaits for my losing,

Slipping, nipping …sipping…toddling.

Scared I'll hit the liquor bottle,

     …nonstop!

Schlepped off then to an early burial.

Screw that scenario!

Strip mall has a super-duper summer sale.

Swear I'll be there without fail!

Swimming

Sky blue water is my capsulation.

Sport training is not a vacation.

Sensations of fluid movements embrace.

Struggle to be a winner is my race.

Self-disciplined I keep up my pace.

Scoreboard later will show first place.

    sensual waves in motion,

      blend with my emotions.

Swaying me as I surge forward.

Sailing above the frothy sea is an ocean bird.

Scooping up a fish for supper.

Splashing fins are heard

    going skyward ...upward.

Saturated by the liquid *azul* ocean

Sounds and sights from sea to shore

Swimming and training I enjoy even more.

Surrounded by water in motion.

Swirling,

    whirling,

        spiraling.

Speed of strokes steadfast.

Stopwatch keeps me on task.

Striving to place; not to be last.

Success strived for in a pool

or in cool ocean water.

Swept all the meet records in the past.

So what if I come in last.

Swimming is an addiction of mine!

Standpoint is...there's no finish line

except the end of my time!

Tattoos

Ticklish tats surround your body.
Torso covered in front and back.
Toes to your head tracing spaced lines.
Tangent touching mystical signs.
Tactile touches tickle when naughty.
Teasing fingers tracking down

> up and around

Targeting sensitive tinted skin.
Touching delivers squirms and shivers.
Thrilling transmitted laughing sound

> giggles and wiggles.

Titillated contact stops to be unwound.
Transition toward a tranquil state.
Truce for another time to wait.
Tickle tactics teaser temptress on a rewound.
Transparent question she asks...
Tell me when muscles and skin do age...

> sagging

> shrinking

> creasing

> drooping

> wrinkling

> withering

Then those aged fleshy tats will look like what...

> from head-to-toe-to-ass?

258

Thanks Coach

Enter fairyland with me,
Fluffy snow white clouds above I see.
Shinning through is my hero.
Taught me to never accept zero.

Coached my running from a thru z.
Gave me my ultramarathon key.
Practice after practice was told what to do...
Sprint the oval track
Attack the shoreline by the sea.
Never look back.
Forefront is where you are to be.
Attack the road with spirit bold.
Pound those miles into mother earth.
Wisp the wind around.
Hear only the breathing sound,

                    racing,

                        pacing,
Ran to the beat of your spirit leading,

                            beating.

                                winning.
Later basking on Florida's sand,
Recalling those behind who were shadowed by my ass

                                as I ran past
Thankful I did not come in last.

                    Dedicated to:
                    Coach Bill Squires

                        259

U.F.O.ers

Ursa minor visitors are exploring earth.

Uncertain as to why humanoids gamble.

Unlucky bets of no valuable worth.

Ulterior greed is one revealed sample.

Unfair negative odds against them exist.

Unfavorable losses occur against their wish

        still ignored as they abide

        no cautionary guide

        playing the game

        losing all the same

        tested for insane.

Urges of the psych possess them to play more.

Universally Earth's addicted aliens don't score.

Unintelligent race these human species are.

Unstable drunken fools at bars.

Uptight speeding fast in their cars

Useless, wasteful gambling day and night

Unwilling to stop eating all in sight

Upheaving each and every bite.

Unstopping smoke vapors noses never cease.

Unqualified to keep their planet at peace

Ultimately in this case, we will abandon this race.

Unanimously all other planets voted the same.

Unconditionally we blast off to space's home base.

Video Games

Video games often become an addiction.

Viewing with emotions creating friction.

Value judgment made with full attention.

Varying attacks from ground to airily.

Vaporizing the enemy in each scenario

Vacillating from which way to turn.

Vengeance to victims lacks concern.

Vile villains slain left no one to beckon.

Vetoed a right-hand turn to move left.

Viewpoint changes second to second.

Vigilantly watching every move.

Vulnerable to one mistake to lose

followed by "selfie boos".

Wrinkles of Today

Wrinkles are nature's way to say
When age is gauged each passing day.
Whatever creases made are yours to stay.
Wealth may buy surgery,

                sculpting by reducing fine lines.
Which will need revision with time.
Well-preserved faces and bodies often are genetics.
Wonderful, if that's your natural cosmetics.
Weapons used by slathering creams on,
Wherefore may reduce lines so fine,

              but isn't a magical wand sign.
With all lines gone,
Worry creases you create when you're down and frown

        slanting

          descending

        angling

          drooping

            downward.
Well, no one likes facts as they sound.

        Just look around.
Wisdom is--winning from within the plastic race.
Win-win situation is to grin from ear to ear.
With graceful beauty is passionate fashion.
Wellbeing is just to accept your loveable smiling face!

262

X's For Face Lift

X marks the spots with little black dots,

    where the surgeon will cut.

    Scalpel slashes through the facial skin

      money, honey, bought you a new face.

X-rayed before and all's in place

    surgery has begun on your case.

      money paid

    Too late to change your mind.

    Incisions have been made

    to tighten up each line

    face lift pulling up every aging sign.

Bandages weeks later removed, stripped away.

Like it or not – your face is a new version of you today

exchanged for another look only a few years to stay .

Like it or not, you paid and paved your way.

Future sagging and lines will come anyway,

little by little everyday.

Aging will never stop.

Opting to try it again?

You're way over the bend.

Why, when you're so near to life's end?

263

Yardsales

*Y*ardsales all day long.

Year-round I go humming a song.

Yesterday I bought gifts for all

             even a soccer ball.

Yielded to temptation at each location,

                 choosing with care for those on my list.

Yard loaded with items for all not to miss.

Yuletide searching for seasonal gifts to wrap.

Yet these finds will fill out my budget gap.

                    Found tree ornaments as well.

                    I won't tell; if you won't tell.

                    Car's loaded now time to leave.

Yours truly, is all set before the eve.

Yesterday's Wrinkles

Yesterdays were here and faded away.

Years fleeting by

       leaving creases that never ceases.

Young no longer, no more.

       face has aged with wrinkled lines.

Yet time, to me, has been so kind.

       Allowing me to be loved,

       by one, who to my facial lines is blind.

Yes, his loving heart shows how divine

       even of youth left behind with time.

Yes, eternity must be sublime.

Zenith Lifestyle

Zinfandel wine in my hand.

Zephyr wind swirling sand.

Zonking out, in a hammock drifting.

    Getting a sun tan,

        while sniffing

           my "special stuff"

             in my buff.

Zero won at the casino table.

    Chilling out from my losses today.

    Maybe I'll smoke some weeds.

Zest for addictions that meet my needs

    gambling

    smoking

    drinking

    snorting

Zilch concerns for whatever others say

    Nor their label.

    Sitting on my ass...

Zealous to have life my way.

    For now, another bottle,

Another glass...

as long as I last.

        Best to rest 'til morrow.

        Hoping I won't lose my ass.

        Money I'll have to borrow.

        Then to the casino again.

        Playing as long as I can.

        Ending living my way

        Every day to make another ten.

Zing-a-linging to life's end.